MY ZOO WORLD
(If All Dogs Go to Heaven,
Then I'm in Trouble)

by

Joanne Faries

My Zoo World
(If All Dogs Go to Heaven,
Then I'm in Trouble)
By
Joanne Faries

Copyright 2011 Joanne Faries

Acknowledgements

I dedicate this book to George & Juanita Crowther. My parents instilled the love of reading and writing.

Much love and thanks to my husband, Ray Faries - so supportive and laughs at my words even as he wields a red pen.

Kudos for home town long distance support - Lori, David & Cherie, Joan, Helen, Lisa, Mary Ellen, Terri, Trish, Debbie, & Natalie

Appreciation goes to so many other friends and family spread all over the USA

Thanks to Texas friends and family, and a special mention to Trinity Writers' Workshop

Table of Contents

Prologue: Mere Kibble

"Thou shall not bring a four-legged creature into our home."

These words were not uttered at my wedding, but it is an unspoken vow. It is part of the prenuptial agreement talk Ray and I had prior to our marriage. My psychic anxiety continues to rear its ugly head and a fear of creatures, great and small, is a factor in my life story. My sister, Lori, vouches for me. She is a product of the same mother who said, "Don't pet the icky dog." My brother, David, is an aberration and has allowed cats into his life. I will include him in my tale, but only because he succumbed to pressure. He will support my claims, yet he is a traitor to the true cause.

Ray reassures me constantly that he is fine with no animals. As youngsters, his boys clamored for a dog to deaf ears. I always said, "You can have as many dogs as you want once you move out." Indeed, now, Kevin, and his wife, Maria, own two big dogs. I don't visit them very often. The other son, Chris, does not have any animals but that is not due to a lack of love for them. I don't visit him much either, just to practice.

After eighteen years of marriage and a slight detour with fish, lizards, a turtle, and a guinea pig babysitting episode, the house remains fur-free. Now if only I could gather friends that are animal-free. But no, that's not to be. Whether through work, a writer's group, or school, I strike up a conversation that turns into friendship. The social escalation ultimately ushers in a home visit or a drive-by pick-up. Then the challenge begins.

I walk up to the front door and ring the bell. An up-roar ensues. Barking, the clatter of paws bang against the door, and I hear a distant, "Get back…get back." Muffled noise. A child's name is called to come get the dog. I stand there and listen to the cacophony. Finally, click and the door is opened a crack. "Hey, Killer wants to meet you." The door is opened wide while a scuffle occurs in the background. "C'mon in." Inwardly I sigh and enter, prepared for the inevitable leap, sniff, and bark test. I pass muster with minimal licks and vow to set up an off premise rendezvous point the next time.

I live with an unforgivable affliction. I'm afraid of animals, not trusting their instincts, knowing they want to bite. I don't want a pet. I don't want to love them, touch them, sit with them, or look at a roll of pictures of them. I don't hate animals. I'm perfectly fine with animals in a zoo, and I admire Jane Goodall and others for their animal efforts. I even sponsored a zoo creature as a present for my father.

Mine is an embarrassing problem. It was never a topic on Oprah. There is no sympathy for someone with my condition. I keep my secret hush-hush. However, when confronted with an animal situation I suck it up, smile, and hide inner turmoil. It is inhuman to not love and embrace animals. It is a dog eat dog world and I'm mere kibble.

Chapter 1: Goats and Llamas, and Puppies, Oh My!

There's always one snotty nosed kid crying at a happy childhood event. Whether it is a birthday party, a circus, or a water park, amidst the gaiety, clamor, and screams of laughter one child hovers in a corner and sobs. Shoulders heave and the red-faced child cannot be calmed or comforted.

I was that four-year old child in the middle of the petting zoo at Plymouth Meeting Mall. My hapless parents beckoned me. It was okay to leave, but I stood rooted in the middle of sawdust hell and wailed. A goat calmly chewed my left shoelace and a llama nibbled on my buttons. My grubby hands wiped my eyes and the smell of stale feed assailed my nose. I whimpered. I was trapped and it was my own fault and I vowed to listen to my mother the next time she said I wouldn't like something. She was right, but I had been persuaded by my father to be brave. He bought my ticket and gave me an encouraging push through the turnstile entrance to my petting zoo debut and debacle.

Every year, the zoo arrived at Plymouth Meeting and I'd gaze at delighted children hugging furry creatures, whose sloppy tongues lapped up any food crumbs in the vicinity. I thought I wanted to put my coin in the slot, turn the dial, and have pellets of something indeterminable pour into my outstretched hand. I perceived that I was on the outside looking into a magical world of laughter and joy. Instead my mother yanked my arm and dragged me away from the fenced area. "Phew, this place stinks," she'd exclaim to my father and with nary a backward glance she'd lead us to the other end of the mall.

In my formative years, I was open to a possible encounter with obviously trained beasts. Teensy fears gnawed at me, but I was willing to put them aside to be like other kids. Dad and I followed behind Mom and I asked him in a small voice, "Can I pet some animals? Mom doesn't have to come."

"Are you sure you want to do that?" Dad asked.

I nodded and my stomach churned, excited yet afraid. He turned to my mother who flicked through a rack of blouses. "I think Joanne and I are going to stroll back to the petting zoo. She wants to visit the animals and I think it is a good idea."

"Oh dear," Mom said without turning around, "are you sure? That pen looked like a germ-fest. She won't like it. You know that."

"Not necessarily. She needs to try new things and this might be fun for her. You have her afraid

5

of her own shadow sometimes. This is an adventure."

My mother pulled a blue shirt from the rack and surveyed my father and me. Her pinched mouth said it all. She did not approve and I started to doubt my desires. My father hung tough and before I could waver she moved over to the next rack. "That's fine. I'll finish and follow soon."

She bent down. Her solemn green eyes met mine. "You can change your mind once you're there. Have fun and I'll see you shortly."

Imbued with a sense of doom, I gave her a hug and then took my dad's hand. He swung my arm and chatted about people as we walked the length of the mall. My chest unclenched and I felt exhilarated. I made a choice, had an opinion, and I was going to see it through. I would hug a goat and pet a llama. This was an exotic island and I would tame the creatures with gifts of food.

The place was bedlam and there was a line. I waited my turn, ticket in hand, and kept my Dad in view. Other kids climbed the fencing. One youngster in overalls managed to shimmy a rail and was astride an unhappy llama. A zoo worker promptly hoisted him off and back over the fence to wait in line like everyone else. I shuffled my feet and allowed a few kids to jump ahead of me. Dad came up beside me for a final word of encouragement, "Go on, give the man your ticket and here's a dime for the feed machine. I'll stand right there." He pointed over my shoulder. With that, he nudged me into the corral, my ticket torn in two, ten cents to spend.

6

I blinked. Kids pushed and shoved towards the biggest animals. There was an area with puppies. It was crowded and I could hear yaps. Something wet licked the back of my leg and I jumped and started moving. A zigzag trail through the petting zoo, and I hadn't touched a single animal on purpose. Up on tiptoes, I looked for my Dad. He gave a reassuring wave. I clutched my dime and decided to spend it. Another line and finally a clink, clunk, and turn. My hand could barely hold the largesse. I turned, smiling, and was face-to-face with a goat. Greedy lips smacked at my hand. As I tried to put pellets into my other hand, more goats approached. They nibbled at my arms, licked up remains on my shirt, and sought pieces I'd dropped in my startled state.

Paralyzed, I brushed the remaining food I hadn't spilled out of my hand thinking that would clear creatures from my personal area. Instead, goats and llamas pushed in closer. Lips opened and revealed large teeth. Hot animal breath surrounded me and I tried to not breathe the stink. Saliva sprayed and I felt sticky and gooey. I crumpled into a ball, but the view from the ground was far more frightening than standing up. Knobby goat knees bumped me. Something gnawed my hair and I flung my hand up to brush it away. Tears singed my eyes. Near the ground, the straw and sawdust emanated the smell of pee. This wouldn't do. I stood up, my hands covered my face and I bawled. I couldn't stop crying, couldn't move my feet because goats trapped me, chewing vociferously on my shoelaces. I was sure I bled. The tingle of nibbles registered in my brain and I couldn't feel my right arm.

Disheveled and alone, I wept. My shoulders shook. I felt shame and fear as a llama scoured my space for food. A teen wearing black jeans and a red shirt hovered over me. "Yo, girly, you want outta here?" I sniffed and nodded. His acne pocked face scowled. Rail thin but wiry, he picked me up with both hands, holding me away from his body. Stiff-armed he whooshed me up and over the fencing to the freedom of the mall. I tapped my feet on tile and relished the fresher air. Woozy from crying, I took the handkerchief my father extended in my direction and blew my nose. He knelt down to tie my soggy shoelaces.

"Well, now you've been to a petting zoo."

"Yep," I snuffled.

I hung my head. My mother tucked my purple shirt into my shorts and gave me a hug. The shirt was damp and stained with remnants of spit and dried food. She didn't hesitate in disgust, just patted me on the back and smoothed my ruffled blonde hair. She did pull out a pack of wet wipes, from her purse that has everything, and proceeded to swipe my hands and face with a damp cloth. Then she handed me a small bag. I reached in and pulled out a toy. It was a stuffed llama.

Chapter 2: Mercy, Mercy, Me

The powerhouse four – Scanlons with twelve kids, McGlyns with ten, Piefers had six, and the Murphys also with six kids – ruled the gangs of Oakland Place. Then there was me, age nine, one of the few kids standing on the corner for the public school bus, and my baby brother, still at home. I desired the plaid skirt, white blouse, and black knee socks uniform. I yearned to be off on Saint Somebody's day (it was always a Friday) and hated trudging the half block home on those days. Cathy, Claire, Tommy, and others weaved their bikes, mouths grape stained from popsicles, and jeered. "Didja learn anything today? Got homework? We built a fort."

"Can I see it?"

"Sure, if mommy lets you out." They'd laugh and grab somebody's hat or even an empty lunch box, and continue their safety in numbers assault.

I'd run home, bang the screen door, and greet my mother. "No, I don't have homework. See, here's my A on my spelling test. I'm not hungry. Can I go play?"

"Be home by five."

In mere seconds, I'd change clothes, leap our steps, and get my bike out of the garage, careful to not scratch the car with my handlebars. Gliding down our driveway, I'd listen for yells, and turn in that direction. Kids always built forts on the Lukens' wooded property. For some reason, the Lukens never bothered us, and there were bike paths too. I followed voices and soon found a herd of kids seated on stumps. I was surprised to see some older brothers and sisters too. Guess with a school holiday, everyone was a bit bored. Mitchell, a ninth grader, lit a cigarette and pointed to some wood. Danny had his arms crossed.

"Move that to nail up for the doorway."

"No hammer or nails."

"Tommy, go get some out of Dad's toolbox."

"No way."

"Not much of a fort without a door."

The concept of a fort was very open ended. Out of sight from a road, we tended to set a perimeter and that was about it. A fallen tree limb often served as a bench. Somebody would bring a soda or maybe some candy, and we'd share our riches. We weren't at the beer stage yet, and only a few older kids fumbled around with smokes. I hung on the periphery, content to be included.

A crunch sound and the slight whir of bikes attracted our attention. Scott said, "Halt, who goes there?" But his voice cracked, and we all giggled. Some of the O'Mara's joined our conclave. Thirteen kids in their household and every one had that O'Mara look: wraith thin and pale even after summer. A dusting of freckles across the cheeks

10

and nose stood out on their translucent skin. Boy or girl, they had huge brown eyes with thick lashes and a head of warm brown curls, tinged with chestnut. Narrow faced weak chinned heads on frail bodies, the O'Mara's all appeared as if a winter wind could whisk them away. A harsh word and they'd crumple. I never did learn all of their names. Closest to my age was Mary Margaret and Mary Therese, but I rarely played at the O'Mara's because they lived on Swedesford Road, which might as well have been in County Cork, Ireland.

Like the O'Mara kids, their pet dogs were skinny and pale too. One mutt arrived with the riders. He panted, sniffed, and worked his way closer to me. I contemplated leaving, but didn't want to draw attention either. Fortunately, Danny scratched the dog's head and tried to engage it in a game of fetch. Thanks to him, I'd avoided a dog licking and could hang out a bit longer.

My neighborhood was a figure eight. I could ride my bike on the Oakland Place/White Oak loop without shouting in to mom. She could see down yards, through bushes, around clothes hanging on lines, and she always knew if I wasn't where I was supposed to be.

If my friends decided to ride the big circle on Meadowbrook Road through the new neighborhood then I needed to let mom know. I was kinda afraid of steep Jenkins Lane and always found an excuse to avoid that ride. It plummeted straight down and if you didn't swerve correctly, you could crash the curb and land in the narrow creek bed. One kid, Patrick, broke his arm. He missed water and hit rocks instead. And finally, Swedesford Road was the outer limits with too much traffic, sloping shoulders, and no road markings.

I could hear my mom calling my name for dinner, but I dallied to hear what the O'Mara's had to say.

"We got a Shetland pony. You can come see him tomorrow, if you want, or ride for a quarter. Ten o'clock." There was a murmur of talk, excited questions, and I had to leave. How big was the pony? How long were the rides? Accompanied or not? Imbued by a mixture of curiosity and dread, I slowly picked up my bike and pushed it to the trail. I'd never rode a horse, wasn't sure if I wanted to. The few stories my mother told of her days on the farm never had happy endings.

"Hey, Crowbar (you gotta love the nickname from Crowther, my last name), come over early and we'll ride bikes to the O'Mara's," said Claire, a McGlyn, from across the street.

I nodded. Hey, I was included. I didn't want to be the only kid to not ride. So, I biked home wondering whether to broach the subject at dinner or to wait until morning. I also debated whether I wanted a pony ride at all, or should I just go and hang around, blend in and be cool. I remembered that pony at the petting zoo. I never did get near him since those goats and llamas blocked my way. Even for a pony he was pretty tall.

Mom bustled in the kitchen. The oven door creaked open. I knew what we were having. You could smell it from the garage. Fish stick Friday. "I

12

told you five. You are pushing it, missy. I shouldn't have to call you. Wash your hands and pour your milk."

The decision was made. I'd wait until morning and see how things looked then. Dad loosened his tie, chucked me under the chin, and asked, "Why so solemn?"

"Oh, nothing. I was thinking about Saturday. Did you see my spelling test?"

A sunny Saturday morning and I arose to wolf down a bowl of Sugar Frosted Flakes. Dad read his paper while David and I watched cartoons, and Mom slept in. Saturday was her day and Dad, David, and I better be quiet. Instead of lounging in front of the TV today, I got dressed and hovered between the television and the front window. Every time I got up to change the channel, ooh three cartoon choices; I'd stand and stare at the McGlyn's for signs of movement.

My father finally lowered his paper. "What are you looking at? You're a jumping bean today."

"Well, a whole group was invited to the O'Mara's. They got a pony and are charging for rides. Claire said she'd come get me. I have a quarter from allowance, and I was hoping you'd say yes. We'll ride bikes and cut through yards and look both ways to cross Swedesford. Please?"

My four-year-old brother, David, echoed my plea. He was on his stomach, still in his pajamas, rolling a Tonka truck over some blocks. "And no,

David, it's for us big kids." He promptly rammed his truck into my ankle. I rubbed it, but ignored him.

"I assume your mother doesn't know about this?" he asked and I shook my head. "Well, I suppose it's fine. Lord knows there's enough older O'Mara's to supervise all of you. Better get your sneakers on. Here comes Claire, I'll roll up the garage so you can get your bike."

"Thanks, Dad." I grabbed my socks and shoes and shot out the front door.

Five McGlyns, three Murphys, a sprinkling of Scanlons, me and a few other tag-a-longs joined in the convoy to the O'Mara's. We rode through the McGlyn's yard and then had a single file trail past the house behind them. Bacon aromas wafted in the breeze. A dog barked but nothing else stirred and we made it to Swedesford. Cars whipped by us on their way to the hardware store or the post office for Saturday morning chores. We double checked both ways and then hurled ourselves across to start the ride up the O'Mara's stony driveway. The crunchy gravel attracted their large German shepherds who barked and panted at our heels. I concentrated pedaling and felt safe in the middle. Pulling up the rear meant German escorts with large teeth.

I looked around. Tall grass waved in the fall breeze, but it was still shorts weather. Indian summer. Bikes, balls, and other toys were strewn about the yard. A mower was abandoned next to a rusty Oldsmobile on blocks. The hood was up and a skinny O'Mara teen clinked tools and ignored our crew. The house looked crusty and faded white paint flaked from the exterior. The porch sagged and the house groaned from the weight of all the children. I'd been inside one time and was fascinated by rows of bunk beds in each kid room. The dining table had two lazy Susans and there was a huge refrigerator in the garage. Mounds of clothing hid the washer and dryer. The sheer volume of piles of everything gave me claustrophobia and I remember being grateful when I got home to my own neat room.

We continued to pump our bikes past the house to the outer field. There, Mary Catherine, Mary Therese, and four or five other brothers and sisters stood with their Shetland pony. One was brushing it and another was trying to tie pink bows in its mane. The pony kept shaking its head and whinnying.

"This is our new pony, Mercy. Did everyone bring money?"

There was a group affirmative and Mary Catherine walked around with a can for us to plunk our change into. She also had numbers for us to draw so there'd be no fights or disagreements on ride order. They had a plan. The number pull did bring groans from a few. I had number twelve, which was fine. I wanted to see how this worked and also build some confidence. My stomach churned and I had the taste of sour milk in my mouth. I swallowed and watched as Mary Catherine, herself, hopped on the pony first.

There was no saddle and no reins. A frayed rope looped around the pony's head and into Mary

Therese's hand. She clicked her tongue while Mary Catherine jabbed the pony with her bare heels. Did I mention that the O'Mara's are always barefoot? Mercy lowered her head and grazed a bit. Then she started a trot. Mary Catherine laughed and everyone clapped which seemed to confuse the pony. It stopped and Mary Therese yanked on the rope to get it moving again. This didn't look reliable.

Numbers were called and kids hopped on and off Mercy. Mary Therese tired of leading and announced everyone had to rotate turns on horse handling. This unnerved me. I followed Claire and we were over two hours into the morning. The pony glistened with sweat and her eyes rolled a bit. She shook her head from side to side and to my untrained eye, her movements were erratic. Claire handed me the scratchy rope as she hopped up on Mercy.

"Make this a good ride, Joanne. You better have the damn thing run." I was stuck now. I had to see this through, lead the horse for Claire, and then ascend the horse and ride.

By this time, kids who'd had their turn were bored with the pony and were throwing balls, wrestling, and generally running amok. Kids who hadn't ridden yet were antsy and a bit punchy. They ran alongside Mercy to give her little slaps to make her go faster. Chaos ruled. Mary Catherine was gone along with her can of money. Mary Therese had relinquished all authority. Twelve years old, she leaned against the makeshift fence and smoked. Wisps of gray clouds swirled about her head. She was proficient at smoke rings.

I was tentative and Claire dug in her heels. Mercy bolted and she cantered across the field. Claire, taken aback, whooped. She stopped yammering at me and held on to Mercy's mane, all bows unraveled. The group kept up a good pace and then the pony swerved back toward the fence. This surprised me and I must have pulled the rope too hard by instinct. Mercy stopped. Claire almost went head over heels and we all panted for air. The grass tickled my bare legs and I lifted my left knee just in time for Mercy to turn and chomp my upper thigh.

I howled, dropped the rope, and collapsed to the ground. Claire hopped off Mercy and Mary Therese ran to grab the pony's rope and walk her back to the fenced area. Kids encircled me as I cried.

"You're not bleeding," somebody said in a disappointed tone.

I looked down amazed at no blood gush. My leg hurt and you could see the outline of the pony's choppers, but no skin broke. Now I was ashamed, annoyed, but hurt. Kids mumbled that I'd ruined everything. There were still riders to follow, but Mercy was led back to her stall to rest and reflect on her morning. Heck, I hadn't gotten my ride but a pony bit me. I was disappointed, yet relieved.

Someone helped me up and I limped to my bike. My leg was stiff, felt like it didn't belong to me. The imprint looked like dentures. It was an agonizing ride home. Disheveled and puffy eyed, I

17

could picture my Mom. She'd inspect my leg; discuss the clinic and rabies shots. Kids streamed home. I lagged behind and those German shepherds barked farewell, nudging, daring me to fall off my bike, so I could be torn apart and disappear on a Saturday morning.

Chapter 3: Farm Fresh Follies

How did I get to be animal nuts? It all began on a farm.

We laughed as we passed around the faded black/white photograph of 1930s Shutters kids. It was pre-Christmas at my Aunt Jane's and family gathered on her enclosed sun porch. Only it wasn't sunny. This cold December evening hinted at snow or sleet. Rain during the day coated trees and rooftops in a shimmering glimmer of ice. There was a cracking sound and a large branch scratched and clawed at the roof as it rumbled to the ground. Startled we paused mid-conversation, and then resumed our chatter. Mouths full of meatballs and drinks in hand, stories were told, disputed, and exaggerated. We weren't an Irish family for nothing.

Now in my late forties, I stared at the photo and wondered about my mother who gazed pensively at the camera, beseeching someone to save her. A big bow tied atop curls that tumbled to her shoulders. She was nine years old, wore a shift dress, knee socks, and sensible tied shoes. I observed a sad girl standing away from her siblings. She probably had a book hidden in a loft in the barn. There she dodged chores and escaped her surroundings. That girl, my mother, Juanita Mae Shutters, was raised on a farm.

My mother's been gone fifteen years now and I sought answers to questions about her farm life. She had refused to discuss it or tell stories. "I hated the farm, the dirt, and the animals. I couldn't wait to get out of there." That's all I ever heard, but I know her distaste for animals carried over into my life. She instilled her fears and predispositions into me from an early age, and I rarely questioned her. My one foray into a petting zoo proved disastrous. Bike rides and barking dogs scared the crap out of me. As much as I did not take after my mother in looks or personality, I did share the anti-animal trait, and I needed to hear more farm stories.

I used the photo as a prompt, "Other than my mother, everyone else looks happy on the farm. What happened?" The photo showed two-year old Rick, a sturdy boy with a dimpled chin and squinty eyes, hugging a large lab/collie mix dog. Rick wore jeans and was barefoot. Jane, age ten with dark hair, was in patched play clothes, not a dress. Finally, ramrod straight in a saddle, sat Lee, eldest at fourteen. A good-looking lad, his wavy hair blew in a breeze and he smiled. It was the late 1930s and the Shutters kids were assembled outdoors on a summer afternoon with tall grasses and a fence as backdrop. There's a rough and tumble quality to the photo and I could picture my Uncle Lee galloping away, Uncle Rick roughhousing with the dog, and Aunt Jane cheering him on.

I flapped the photo to get everyone's attention. "I need stories, folks." Uncle Rick leaned forward in his chair and reminisced.

"If you were ever kicked by a mule, you'd hate animals too." Uncle Rick claimed my mother never trusted animals after that incident at a young age. "You can see from the photo, Nites (Juanita = Nita = Nites) was a girly-girl. She wore dresses and hated to get dirty. Face it, on the farm you get dusty."

Aunt Jane agreed. "Juanita complained the whole time we'd gather eggs. She'd dance around and yelp. Yes, those hens would peck you, so you had to use a stealth method. Sneak up, slide the hand in and out, and voila, an egg. She'd moan and groan, such a huge commotion."

She continued, "Ew, but it stinks your mom said and would hold her nose. Another chore involved stirring fresh milk. She'd gag and mess around. Nites was hopeless on the farm and couldn't wait to grow up."

My younger sister, Lori, chimed in, "Chicken fluffing sounded worse."

"What the heck was that?" I asked. Obviously I missed a few chapters on my mom's life story. However, I was getting a better picture of her life on the farm, and frankly I agreed with her. I'd never have cut it there myself. Ugh.

"Oh, Mom told me about it," Lori said. " In the summertime, on a typical muggy Pennsylvania August day, you had to go to the henhouse and rustle the chickens in their nests. Get them stirred up. The ones that didn't move, you marked the expiration date, and had to pull them out."

"Yuck," I grimaced.

"Blech, indeed," my Aunt Jane said. "It was gross."

"I'd have never survived farm life," I said. "No wonder Mom never liked cooking chicken either. I have to say raw chicken grosses me out. Ray's my poultry chef."

"Yes," Aunt Jane said, "you are very much like your mother on this one. You, too, Lori."

My brother, David, piped up, "I can't say I'd have wanted to do the chores, and my allergies would have killed me, but I'm okay with animals."

Lori and I hooted. "Yeah, like you'd have milked cows and shoveled manure."

My father laughed. "None of you kids were born to be cowpokes. Your mother made sure of that."

"Wasn't there a Shetland pony?" I asked. I continued my line of questioning. Might as well cover all animals. We'd already dismissed chickens and cows, and I knew about her fear of dogs.

"Ah jeez. That was a miserable horse," said Uncle Rick. "Whatever Nites told you was true." He and Aunt Jane talked over each other.

"I forget its name…"

"…I wanted to forget its name. That little pisser would try to rub you off at the fence or a tree or wherever it could."

"Yeah, or gallop and then halt. Whiplash. Sheer orneriness…"

"…fat, too. Spoiled by our mother, your Nana. Remember she always wore those plaid farm work dresses. Big apron, too, with deep pockets…."

"…sugar cubes or carrots. That damn horse scarfed up handfuls."

"She'd keep the pony brushed and even tie our old ribbons in her mane."

Uncle Rick finished, "We hated that pony. Your mother was absolutely correct."

"Now Buzz was our main work horse. He was steady, at least for me," said Aunt Jane.

"Seemed like Lee always chose Buzz if Dad wasn't on him. I rarely got to ride since I was so much younger," mused Uncle Rick. "After the mule incident, and that mean Shetland nipping at Nites, she was done with horses. She never fought to ride Buzz."

Aunt Jane said, "Your mother was happiest if she got to visit Aunt Betty in town. No animals jumping up on her, and no chores. She liked to shop or go to a movie. Those were big treats."

My father said, "Your mother always looked out of place on the farm. She never talked about it much. Didn't have a 'funny animal' story to share or a 'hey, this happened today in the barn' story. I learned to not even ask."

"You might want to talk to your Uncle Lee," said Aunt Jane. "He might have something to add."

"I'll do that. You've helped me a bunch. I figured the farm affected Mom and she passed it on to us kids. It's kinda odd, you know, to be farm bred and dislike animals."

Everyone laughed, grabbed dinner plates, and moved on to other subjects.

I talked to Uncle Lee later that week. He'd retired in Florida. I hadn't seen him in awhile, but the last time I saw him I did a double take. In his seventies, wearing jeans and plaid shirts, he looked so much like my Pop-Pop, his father. All he needed was a pair of suspenders and a pipe. Uncle Lee even walked like him, as best as I remember Pop-Pop before he died. Shoulders hunched, in no hurry, Pop-Pop would amble down the sidewalk as I'd run, jump, and prattle beside him.

"Yeah, I'd ride Buzz a lot," Uncle Lee told me. "He was a good horse. But your mother... now she was scared of everything on that farm, you know." I murmured in agreement and encouraged him to tell more. "She was always getting stung by a bee, nipped by the Shetland, pushed over by our big collie. I'm thinking our old mule kicked her, too. She bruised easily and also hated to get dirty. Nites never slopped the pigs or entered that pen or the sheep's area."

"What did she do at the farm?" I asked.

"Oh she loved to read and would take a book out by the creek. She was like you kids. Nites was excited when we moved to town after Dad retired."

"Well, I appreciate the stories. Anything else you can think of let me know."

24

"I can tell you about the last time I saw Juanita on a horse. She was out in the field and I think Dad picked her up and put her on Buzz. Something spooked him and bam, Nites was thrown off. It was a Sunday or a holiday with lots of company around. Charlie, a friend of Uncle Wally, took off running across the field. Should've seen him. Big old guy, 'bout 6'3" lumbered to scoop her up. She was fine, just shook up. He tried to put her back up on Buzz, but she pitched a fit. Swore she was never riding again. And she didn't. Your mom was stubborn. She never saddled up again." He paused as if to reflect back and be sure. "Nope, never again."

So, like my mother, a Shetland pony nipped me. I'd never been thrown off a horse, but Buttercup (future chapter) certainly attempted to bounce me off a tree. Dogs have always been an issue. Guess I need to keep my eye out for kicking mules. And I certainly don't plan to move to a farm anytime soon.

Chapter 4: Pixie and Poodles

"No, don't. Stay away from that dog."

"No, that's dirty, go wash your hands."

Everyone blames her mother for something. Thus when I'm called to appear on a talk show, I will accuse my late mother, "Juanita Shutters Crowther instilled a fear of animals in me." My sister, in the audience, will nod and answer in the affirmative when the host addresses her. "Yes, it was ingrained. Stay away from animals. Don't go near them. You'll catch rabies." The host will roll her eyes and no doubt bring out dogs as evidence of sanity.

Rabies, tetanus, and other reasons for shots – all could happen if you messed with animals. Every so often, a rumor zoomed through our neighborhood that a _____(fill in the blank – dog, cat, skunk, squirrel) had rabies. Unlike other kids who, armed with a slingshot or BB-gun, roamed the streets seeking the froth-at-the-mouth diseased creature, I crossed to the opposite side of the street at the sight of a suspicious animal. Ever vigilant, I'd look over the yard before I'd run out to play. Never know when a crazed squirrel could bound from a tree in a rabies-induced frenzy.

Dirty, messy, nasty. Avoid animals. That was the message I heard from the womb. I didn't question it and was not put in situations at an early age to overturn my mother's credo. There was many a bike ride around the block ruined by fearsome German shepherds. Schroeder and Bach ruled White's Road. They barked and nipped at my legs that churned furiously by their house. No leash laws or electronic fences existed in the late sixties.

The phone rang one night during dinner and it was my Aunt Jane. In a hushed conversation, my mother learned that the neighbor's dogs attacked my cousin, Gary, age eleven. Not invited to the hospital, my imagination ran wild with the word "mauled". Later I saw Gary's facial scars and that was enough to reinforce my fears.

Did he tease the dogs? Something caused them to turn and attack. In family lore, the neighbor kids and dogs trotted along in the field. Gary ran to catch up with them and the dogs might have been surprised and lashed out. No one can confirm the story. The external scars faded, but for me an internal scar remained. Never assume a dog won't attack. It's in an animal's nature to protect itself. Mom's right, you never know what a creature will do.

Then there was Pixie, Aunt Jane's dog. This little mutt terrier, which looked like Toto, could levitate in the garage; leap straight up and hang in the air. She yapped from dawn to midnight. I swear we could hear her as mom turned off Sumneytown

Pike and drove down the lane to Aunt Jane's house. We'd pull into their driveway and the dog would go berserk. They certainly did not need an alarm of any sorts. Pixie announced arrivals loud and clear. Nonetheless, Mom would honk the horn to let Aunt Jane know we were in her driveway. Aunt Jane knew the drill. She'd come out, wave, and then tie up Pixie's lead by an extension or two to rein in the little terror.

Pixie strained at her leash until you'd think she would die from strangulation. Then when you'd walk to the garage back door, practically slinking by like a cat burglar, Pixie extended herself with every inch of her being and nipped your ankles. She was snarky and lived long past normal dog years.

Now, my Uncle Lee, Aunt Audrey, and cousin, Sandy, had miniature poodles. Equally as yappy, they did behave or Aunt Audrey would put them in the laundry room, where they'd claw, whimper, and annoy. Oh they'd try to jump up and beg for treats, matching bows in their hair, little poodle tails twitching. I was not fond of those dogs, and thus did not do many sleepovers with my cousin.

My mother's influence ran deep. I didn't yearn to pet dogs, play with cats, or appreciate animals. Nipped on the finger by Pippie, my cousin Robert's guinea pig, I lost interest in watching her spin her wheel. The few times I went over to a neighbor's for lunch and the cats walked on the counter, nosing the food, I regretted seeing meal

28

preparation. Better to not know what goes on behind swinging doors.

I've lived away from my hometown more than half my life. My mother's been gone over fifteen years. Nevertheless her voice niggles in my brain. "Oh, yucky. Don't go near that dog."

"Wash your hands."

"Careful, we don't know that animal. It's not from our neighborhood."

"Rabies shot."

Chapter 5: Pixie Weighs In

First the name Pixie doesn't do me justice. I'd much prefer Sheena, Mistress of Mayhem. I'm more than a runty dog and deserve respect.

Second, the kid's got skinny legs and she hops around so much that I have to leap to keep up with her. Joanne claims I yap. Well, you should hear her squeal. The pitch hurts my ears.

We don't get many visitors out here in Harleysville. My pre-teen boys, Mark and Gary, ride bikes, play football, and they never want me to join them. I'm miniature but scrappy and I play rough. Their friends avowed I used my teeth, so I was banished from any sports events. It's frustrating. I'd love to run free in the fields, but neighbors claim I bark too much and upset the cows.

If we do leave the house, we go to the Dairy Queen but I'm not allowed out of the car. There's some stupid rule that dogs aren't permitted on the miniature golf course. The one time I was tied up near the picnic tables, I barked and scared a pig-tailed girl. She dropped her Dilly Bar and ran crying to her parents. I licked up that ice cream as

30

fast as my tongue could slurp. It was worth the extra swat on the nose for that escapade.

So, most of the time I'm tied up in our garage and enjoy a decent piece of concrete real estate. Gene, master of all, departs early in the morning for work or golf or both. He's gone a lot. Jane's VW Bug is parked out of my reach. That's fine. I try to piddle near the passenger door where the boys can track it in. Ssshh! That's between us.

If we do have company, it's Jane's sister with her kids. Sheesh, the mom's a wreck. She pulls into the driveway in that ugly Ford station wagon with the fake wood trim. Blasts the horn, which gives me the jitters. I have to bay because Jane might not have heard the horn. The wagon idles in the driveway. No one exits the vehicle until Jane bustles out, yanks my rope tighter by a length or two, and gives the all clear sign. I'm wound up by this time, eager to see some new faces, play a game, or at least get petted. I avoid growling. Instead, I aim for a pleasant mid-tone bark indicative of my happy demeanor. I plead to be untied.

No love from this crew. They act like fugitives slinking up against the garage wall. I stretch and strain to reach them, to lick a welcome, and I yelp all of my news. The young lad, David, might reach out a hand towards me, but his mother hurries him out of my reach. That leaves Joanne, knobby knees and all. She's kinda clumsy and often misjudges my distance reach. If I do my pounce leap and yap at the same time, I can generally get a swipe in.

"Ow, Pixie bit me," the kid will tattle.

31

It was only a nip and I didn't draw blood. I will say that Jane defends me. "Pet Pixie once and she'll leave you alone."

No I won't, but it's a nice thought.

Chapter 6: Stuffed in a Closet

A six foot long purple snake slept on my bed the majority of my pre-teen years. As a toddler, I was featured on the family Christmas picture card snug in my jammies and leaning on a huge stuffed puppy dog. Glassy eyed creatures sat on bedroom shelves, propped in playroom corners, and served as confidantes when needed. Pandas, bears, a lion, sheep, and even a turtle were stuffed animals that my mother could not resist. She might have hated the farm, but she loved a toy store and could not withstand the lure of plush gifts.

My father would roll his eyes, "Don't the kids have enough animals?" and my mother responded, "Oh, but this one is so cute."

Hey, the stuffed animals didn't make a mess; they were colorful: and they did bring joy, especially to Mom.

A month before Christmas and I studied for my first semester exams, wrote papers, and worked my part-time jobs. Lived at home and commuted to Temple University, still enjoyed Mom's cooking when I was there, and could spend time with Lori. Ten years younger than me, eight-year old Lori was my own live action doll. She walked, talked, and yes, adored me. As her big sister, I could do no wrong and I liked her company. We'd go to the mall or a park, and I'd attend some of her school plays or special functions. By the time the third kid rolls around, the novelty has worn off, so Mom was fine with me picking up any slack.

A chilly Tuesday afternoon and I was between class runs. Decided to stop home for a late lunch or early dinner. Mom flung open the front door and watched me gather books and slide out of the car. Sun glare on the glass storm door blocked her features. Smile or frown? I couldn't remember if I'd forgotten to do something. I hurried up the front walk and heard the click and whoosh of the storm door, "C'mon! I need your help before Lori's school bus pulls up."

I relaxed, ducked inside to dump my load on the kitchen table, and watched my mom scurry to get car keys. Like an Irish pixie, my mom moved fast. Her reddish gray hair in a neat curly bob suited her pale complexion, now flushed with the freckles heightened by her excitement. Tiny and quick, she was out the garage door in a flash and hollered back, "Follow me. It's in the trunk."

She popped the trunk and wedged inside was a humongous stuffed brown bear. His arm, now unhindered by the trunk, stuck up in a friendly wave. An unblinking charcoal eye stared unwaveringly at me and it exuded a twinkly glow.

34

Cheery grin on his face and a jaunty blue and red striped cap clinched the deal. Big Teddy would be a hit under the Christmas tree.

My mother vibrated. She shuffled from foot to foot and looked over her shoulder for the school bus. I glanced at my watch; we had a minimum of fifteen minutes to act.

Now my mom chattered, " This was on sale at the grocery store, believe it or not, and I couldn't resist. One of the bagboys helped stuff him into the trunk. I abandoned my food cart in favor of Big Teddy. He's too big for me to carry upstairs by myself. I'm so glad you came home between classes." She gave me a hug. "What do you think?"

We stood there and stared into the trunk. Scenes from various mob movies flashed before my eyes.

I deliberated. "We need something to cover him."

"You're right," she said and dashed into the house. I barely had time to pull Teddy from the trunk when she returned with a garish flowered sheet. We proceeded to wrap him tight like a mummy.

"Where do you need me to carry him?" I asked. My mother had all afternoon to ponder this question and she responded quickly.

"Your closet, the one with summer clothes. I moved a few things around. I knew you wouldn't mind, and we can set him on the upper shelf." I shrugged, picked up my unwieldy bundle, and proceeded to waddle into the house. The bear wasn't heavy, but he was bulky and the sheet

35

wanted to unravel. I struggled up our narrow stairs and into my room for a breather. Mom opened the closet door and I could see she'd moved some luggage and other non-essential items.

"I think I hear the bus. Damn." She never cursed. "The bus is early. Can you get the bear up on the shelf yourself? I'll go distract Lori." With that, my mother zoomed out of my room and closed the door behind her. Man, she was wired. She loved Christmas and worked hard to surprise us all with the perfect treat.

I tucked pieces of the sheet back into the mummy wrap and proceeded to heave Teddy into the closet. He wanted to tumble off the shelf, and I had to give an extra shove to ensure he stayed intact, didn't dangle precariously on the ledge.

I could hear Mom ask Lori questions about her day, and the fridge door opened and closed. With a final reassuring pat to Teddy, I shut the closet and then rearranged my face to not reflect the last half hour of excitement. Rounding the kitchen doorway, my mother caught my eye and I gave a slight nod. She smiled and turned back to Lori's spelling test, while I fixed a sandwich prior to my night class.

Any other time of the year, Lori would never be around when I opened closet doors. The countdown to Christmas proved tricky. She lingered. She hovered. I think she sensed a magical being encased in a cloth garden, a magnetic pull from Teddy's chocolate brown eyes.

The buildup was excruciating. By Christmas Eve, my mother could barely contain her glee, and

36

even my father was ready for Christmas Day. He was happy he didn't have to assemble anything. Finally, Lori was tucked into bed and asleep with the proverbial visions of sugarplums, and Mom and I tip toed to my room. I pulled on the sheet and woke Teddy from his winter's nap. His ear was slightly scrunched, but other than that his eyes sparkled and his open arms beckoned a hug.

Mother inspected him for matted fur or any other imperfections. This was the present from Santa and Teddy had to be in superb condition. With muffled whispers and a slight stumble on my part, I hauled Teddy downstairs. Mom placed him in the corner. "Do you think that's the right spot, George?" she asked my father. Dad stood munching on a Christmas cookie and watched her walk back and forth. She tilted her head, she scrunched down to be in Lori's sightline, and she angled Big Teddy one last time. Straightened his big red bow and patted him on the head. Satisfied she announced it was bedtime.

I slept longer than expected and was surprised that the house was so quiet on Christmas morning. Stretched, slid out of bed, donned my robe, and peered out my window. It's a habit. Have to look for snow on Christmas morning. No snow, but a glorious sunshine day. I padded down the steps and joined my mother on the landing. "Ssh! Take a look." Nestled in Teddy's arms, Lori was asleep. She celebrated Christmas morning early.

Chapter 7: Old Buttercup

"Where's my boots?" Kevin's muffled voice called from his closet, since I sent him to his room to change a grubby t-shirt for a clean one. I walked down the hallway and stuck my head into his room. Two skinny legs poked out from under his bed. I decided to ignore the filthy bare feet, since he planned to cover them up.

"Your father's outside loading the car. Why are you looking for boots?" I asked. In my mind, I envisioned his rubber boots packed in the attic with winter gear.

Kevin came out from under the bed. His fine brown hair stuck out all over the place and his fresh t-shirt was rumpled. Huge brown eyes with long lashes stared at me. In an exasperated tone, he explained, "I need boots to ride." I must have looked blank, because he continued. "I'm seven now and big enough to ride Storm. I won't be stuck on the stupid pony, Belle. With Storm, I can roam the whole pasture." I tuned him out as he continued to discuss the merits of Storm versus the pony, opened the closet, cringed at the upheaval of clothes and toys, and pulled out his boots. They, of course, had been tossed in a closet corner.

"Wow, thanks. How'd you find 'em?"

"I could smell 'em."

He giggled and plopped on the floor to put them on.

"Hey, hey, hey." I snapped my fingers and pointed towards the door. " Take those outside and give them a good clap. I don't want all that dried mud in here." He started to run off. "Don't you need some socks, too?" I pulled open the top drawer and threw him a pair.

I had a moment to think. Since dating Ray, I met his parents and grandparents twice. Both times were at his sister's house in Arlington. I knew Ray's folks owned horses and had seen pictures of their home and land in Waxahachie. The bucolic countryside appeared lovely. Under the current invite for the day, I envisioned a tasty picnic in the backyard and horses gamboling in the field. Based on Kevin's chatter, my serene vision dissolved into an activity filled animal interactive day. However, rather than worry ahead of time, I decided to see how the day flowed. I glanced out the window at the blue skies and fluffy clouds. Not a chance of rain in sight.

Ray announced final countdown. Chris, age nine, and Kevin, seven, scrambled into the truck and buckled up. I took a look around the kitchen, picked up my cake tin, and the flower spray for Ray's mother, and locked the door behind me. We were off to the country.

It was an uneventful trip. The boys kept their squirms and wrangles to a minimum. They somehow knew when to avoid punishment. An hour later, we pulled into the gravel drive and two big dogs barked and ran alongside our vehicle. Ray's father, L.D., grabbed the collars to hold them back. The boys piled out of the car and hugged the dogs before jumping into grandparents' arms. An assortment of relatives arrived. Amid backslapping and greetings amongst families, dogs yapped and cows leaned through the fence to chew grass along the driveway border. I did not spot any horses.

We indeed gathered to eat lunch at picnic tables nestled under a shade tree. No flies, a light breeze blew a faint whiff of manure, but that smell was overwhelmed by the acrid odor of charred burgers. Story telling distracted L.D. Soon enough shooting flames called his attention back to the grill. No matter. Chicken, salads, fresh green beans, potatoes, baskets of biscuits and more kept us seated at the table. Restless, the boys and cousins played tag and wrestled with the dogs. So far, I remained under the radar. Ray's granddaddy snuck nibbles to the dogs, but he sat at the opposite end of the table from me. I was comfortable and content.

Kevin ran up to the table. He was always the appointed ambassador for the kids. His eager grin and enthusiastic energy melted his grandmother's heart and I don't think I'd ever heard her decline a request.

Sure enough, his high-pitched voice, with the right plead tone asked, "Please, please can we ride horses now? We've waited forever and ever. Remember, you said I could ride Storm."

The protests began. "No fair. I want to ride Storm."

"My turn." And so on. My reverie shattered.

Joyce got up and said that everyone would get a turn as soon as we cleared the tables. I never saw kids haul plates and trash so fast. Ray and I shook out the tablecloths and he gave me a hug. "How's your day, dear? I've hardly even seen you."

I hugged back. "Everything's great. So, are you going to ride?" I tried to act nonchalant.

'Of course, that's part of the reason to visit. You'll love it. I bet Mom saddles up Buttercup for you." He walked ahead of me as Kevin and Chris signaled to him to hurry up.

I dragged my heels. Ray knew I wasn't keen on pets, but we had not gone in depth on my various animal fears. We'd been having a fun summer. His boys seemed to tolerate me. Ray cooked a mean batch of sour cream enchiladas. Why appear as psycho girlfriend? I avoided a cow patty and tried to compose my face to appear joyful.

I heard shuffling in the grass behind me and looked to make sure it wasn't a snake. Ray's grandmother caught me and we strolled to the stable. She was a delightful lady and regaled me with a horse story about Ray. "He was all set to be a cowboy, gonna roam the range at age four. Boots, hat, his granddaddy's belt, complete with a huge buckle, looped around his skinny waist 'bout three times, toy pistols, Lone Ranger mask, and his pillow tucked under his arm. He just needed a

41

boost." Laughing, we leaned on the fence and watched as young cousins eagerly hauled saddles from the barn, combed manes, and bribed the horses with carrot treats.

Joyce called my name and indicated I should enter the fence and join her in the barn. I excused myself from grandmother and inched towards a golden tan mare. Joyce cinched the saddle and turned towards me. "Here's Buttercup. She's been around forever and loves people. Ray indicated you don't really ride, so I trust you on Buttercup. She'll know what to do and where to go." I oozed apprehension. She patted the saddle and called to Ray, "C'mere and give Joanne a boost. I need to see if Mother wishes to ride too." Ray hopped off his large black steed. Not to brag, but he looked so cute in his jeans and his borrowed straw cowboy hat as he came over to help me.

I bit my lip. "Darling, give me a brief rundown on what I do." I fought to keep my voice from quivering. Oblivious to my panic mode, he locked his hands to give me a lift. It took two heaves to get my un-coordinated butt into the saddle. I struggled to not list to port.

"Hold the reins. Old Buttercup knows what to do. Follow everybody else. It's a trail ride." Ray patted my leg and jogged back to his horse. Maybe I should have burst into tears and collapsed when I was back at the fence. Now I was stuck. I glanced around. Kevin glowed atop Storm. He had already logged a few miles circling the family, eager to begin the trek. Everyone looked at ease and relaxed. They chatted or called to each other, seated astride equine glory as easily as sitting in lawn chairs. It took all of my concentration to sit and to breathe. I gave Buttercup a tentative pat. She turned her head and gave me a look. The kind of look that said, "I know you are a rookie and you are gonna be sorry. Where's my sugar cube?"

Ray's grandfather took the lead and the ride commenced. Immediately, Ray, Chris, James, Connie galloped ahead. Like poetry, they moved as one with their horses. So smooth, muscles rippled, the pasture grasses waved in the breeze, and laughter floated back to me. It was like out of a commercial.

Old Buttercup and me. I swear I could feel her sigh. Then she decided to stand there and piss. I waited, looked around, smiled to no one, and acted as if this was business as usual for me. I could be at the movies. I could be reading a book. I could…oops. Buttercup abruptly took off. I held on and tried to feel the rhythm. Ouch. This was not comfortable. She hit every pothole (is this the correct terminology for a field?) and swerved towards the fence. I didn't know where to look. I was far behind everyone. I tried to signal distress to the family, watch the fence, view the ground, the sky, hold the reins, grab the saddle horn, decide if I still liked Ray, analyze which way to fall to the ground, figure out if I could get a tissue out of my pocket, then debate on whether I could use the tissue to blow my nose or better to let it run so I'd be a drippy mess at the end of this glorious afternoon.

We veered away from the fence and then stopped to graze a bit. I tried to yell to Ray, "Hey, what about me?" but my cries evaporated in the wind. I sounded weak and puny. Back in pioneer days, I was the one wolves celebrated. They could have licked their chops and not believed their good fortune, as I was separated from the herd without a backward glance. I was left to forage for food or drink; shoeless I wander in the snow.

Enough of that doomsday talk. Hot and sweaty from frustration, I yanked the reins and dug in my heels. What the heck! I'd exert my will. Buttercup turned her head and bared her teeth, I swear. Then she took off. No canter, no trot. This was a full-out run and she aimed for the lone tree in the middle of this pasture. I crouched and held on. My thighs hurt from squeezing. Darn, I wish I hadn't drunk all of that iced tea. Now I needed to pee and this jostling wasn't aiding the situation. My glasses were askew and hair blew every which way. I couldn't see a darn thing save for the looming tree. Where was everybody?

Buttercup kept up a full-court press. For an old gal, she could move. I'd be impressed if it hadn't been my life in danger. She aimed for the lowest branch and I hunkered down and closed my eyes. Leaves brushed my head and I heard some snaps of twigs and then silence. I opened my eyes. Buttercup and I gasped in unison. She flicked her head, tossed her mane like an annoyed teenager who couldn't believe I still invaded her space. I slowly rose up and re-arranged myself on the saddle. I think my underwear was strangling me. I

44

couldn't feel my feet. How long had I been on this horse? Did I reach the end of the Chisholm Trail?

Off in the distance, Ray and family rode towards me. He gave me a big wave. I lifted my hand and composed myself by the time they all trotted by.

"Why are you out here by this tree? We wondered where you got to?"

I gritted my teeth and responded blithely, "Oh, I think Buttercup wanted some shade. How's everyone doing?"

Kevin, still excited, rode by and showed me how Storm could rear up on his hind legs. I mustered a cheer and clapped. I was exhausted and deserved an Academy Award for this performance. Get me off this horse. Buttercup decided to head back to the barn. She willingly followed everyone and behaved. She would win Best Actress. I was merely Best Supporting. At the barn, I did not wait for Ray to help me off. Forget grace, beauty, and proper horse deportment. I scrambled off Buttercup and did not give her a sugar cube. We gave each other a good long look. She knew. She knew that I had not fainted or cried. I wanted to, but I didn't. My legs hurt, all chafed. My back twinged and my butt was sore. However, I walked away from Buttercup without a limp. I had my pride.

The kids were in charge of cleanup, so I could stagger back to the humanity of the house. Soft cushioned sofa beckoned and I collapsed. Ray brought me a glass of lemonade, oblivious to my traumatized condition, and we sat together as

45

everyone re-lived the trail ride adventure. Old Buttercup and I missed forging the creek and seeing a snake. Something I could look forward to on my next date, or in my nightmares.

I lucked out. Ray's folks sold their home and land within a year thanks to the Texas Super Collider project. To the dismay of the boys, the horses and livestock were parted with too. My reputation as a horsewoman was intact, and I did not have to fake illness on any subsequent visits. Oh, and Ray asked for my hand in marriage in 1989 and I said yes.

Chapter 8: Thunder Daze or I Miss Old Buttercup

Cue up the music and sing-a-long. "She's back in the saddle again."

Omni Pro management decided to host a company picnic one year and forego a Christmas party. Ray brought the invitation home to post on the fridge. Barbed wire design outlined the fun planned:

Spread the joy of the workplace to an afternoon at a local dude ranch. Bond with fellow co-workers and their families. Participate in a rousing game of horseshoes, swing on the ropes, and bask in down home country atmosphere. Plenty of food and fun for all. The highlight (!) of the day is a trail ride.

The boys greeted Ray's brochure with appropriate cheers and yipee-ki-yays. I glanced at the calendar and cringed. It had been two years since my ill-fated ride on Buttercup. I was no longer sore and I had chalked it up as a good pre-marriage story. Somehow I had passed a family test, and unbeknownst to Ray I hid my horse terror well. Perhaps too well. Now I had to face my fears amongst his work crew. It's a great batch of people, but they don't need to see me meltdown. Again, why borrow trouble? I told myself to join in the festivities, and maybe the trail ride was optional.

Yeah, right. This was a huge organized event and while I hid in the restroom for a while, I could hear my name. Too late to guzzle another beer. The cowpokes saddled up everyone and a bored black horse turned his head to stare at me. I could see his thoughts expressed in his eyes, "Hey rookie. I heard about you from Buttercup. We're going to have a super ride. I know where all of the potholes are located." It took two tries to heave my butt up on Thunder. He was a lot taller than Buttercup. I swayed in the saddle and listed to port. Some things don't change. Excited chatter filled the air. I heard Kevin's high-pitched voice. Due to my tardiness from the restroom I was near the end of the line of riders, not mingled in with the Omni Pro gang. Restless energy converted to forward motion and we began. I tried to feel the rhythm, gave up, and gripped the saddle and reins. My stomach clenched and I forced myself to breathe. I bit my lip that was chapped from a day in the August sun and hairdryer wind.

Then I questioned myself. Why did I marry Ray? Why didn't I extend my vacation up north to miss his company summer picnic? Finally, was I crazy to attempt the second trail ride of my life? These questions and others rattled through my brain as old Thunder decided to stop and urinate. I gave a tight-lipped smile and nod to riders who passed me. I would have appreciated some sympathy for my plight, but in general, I obstructed the path.

Folks mumbled and kicked their heels into their horses to hurry them past the loser whose horse backed up. I gave a weak tug to the reins and tried a click sound with my tongue. That sound used to work in the few western films I've seen. The horse would respond and he and his rider would gallop away. Thunder was deaf, his eyes glazed over, and he emitted a musty barn odor. For a while I thought my deodorant was not doing its job. I threw horseshoes earlier and worked up a sweat in the sun. However, the odor oozed over the entire trail. It was not good to be downwind.

So, I was on a horse, at a dude ranch outside of Fort Worth, and my group left me. This was not on purpose. I was willing to admit Thunder and I did not stay with our group, but the organizers of this place should have looped us all together. Anticipate what can go wrong and do preventative maintenance. Most of all, I'd hoped my husband would notice I was missing. But he was riding with the boys and all of the commotion that encompassed.

My situation deteriorated. Now, Thunder let loose a huge fart. What do they feed the horses? He started to move and I hung on. At least this trail ride involved an actual trail, not an open pasture like my adventure at Ray's family ranch.

We clopped along and I could hear laughter further up the path though I did not glimpse sight of anyone. An airplane flew overhead. Maybe a search party had been sent to look for me. I was

49

not far from civilization. Surely, we'd catch up soon. The pace wasn't too bad and I relaxed and looked around. Scrubby trees and cactus dotted the parched, beige land. A buzzard circled above, keeping an eye on me. Thunder kicked up dust behind him. I swatted a fly.

Oh no. We came to a fork in the road and Thunder did not seem to know which way to go. How long had he been working here? You'd think he could recognize scenery or scents. Like an ancient Native American, I scanned the two choices for signs of recent activity. Perhaps a dropped water bottle would point me in the right direction. Dry as a bone. Neither trail looked promising and I wondered what would happen if I turned Thunder around and doubled back. There was a monstrous assumption implied in this theory. Did I really think I could bend Thunder to my will and use the reins to speak his language?

While I contemplated choices and my stomach rumbled, Thunder bore to the left. That seemed odd. Perhaps he was left-hoofed and that was a natural inclination. I tend to bear to the left in movie theater entrances. Or maybe this was a large loop trail that ran clockwise. I glanced at my watch. I'd messed with Thunder and this trail for thirty minutes. The whole trail ride was supposed to be an hour. Next up was vittles, grub, or lunch in whatever form you wanted to call it. I'd worked up an appetite and now, ahead of time, decided to be mad if everyone ate without me. The Omni Pro gang was all Type A go-getters, super salespeople. No mercy. I sniffed the air and there was a hint of mesquite smoke barbecue. Either that or I was delirious. Yep, they'd scarf down all the beef and beans in a heartbeat. I'd be left with biscuit crumbs.

Thunder trotted faster and we broke into a clearing. I had dismissed a pasture fiasco too soon. He galloped off the path and headed towards the one tree in sight. My left foot slipped out of its stirrup. In my struggle to recapture it, my right foot flung itself loose. Feet flailed and I gripped my knees tighter. Gnarled branches loomed closer and I closed my eyes, crouched, and held on. He screamed to a halt. I lurched in my seat but stayed aboard. We stood there in the shade. Thunder calmly chewed some grass and I exhaled.

I heard a commotion and here rode Ray with a trail hand who spoke first, " What the heck are you doing? This isn't our property. You can't just ride off the trail and go wherever you want to go."

My scared tears evaporated and now I gulped back angry tears. "You tell that to Thunder. You folks are responsible for him and me. Where have YOU been? Get me off of this horse."

I dropped the reins and Ray scrambled off his horse in time to help me leap off of mine. "Are you o.k.? I'm sorry. I was busy with the boys and lost track of you. I'm really, truly sorry."

I choked out my words, "How far is it to the ranch? I'm hungry and I'm finished with horses." The ranch hand reined in all three and started back to the wooded trail area. Ray waved at him to go on ahead and indicated we'd walk back.

Turned out, Thunder and I were very close to the end of the circuit when he'd seen his chance to break for adventure. On the ride to find me, the young worker told Ray, "No one likes Thunder. He's ornery." Figured I was assigned him. Then again, it made me yearn for my afternoon with Old Buttercup.

Chalk 'dude ranch' off my list of animal adventures. I don't need more horse stories to tell. Subsequent years, Omni Pro held Christmas parties without any reindeer games.

I Don't Miss Old Buttercup or Thunder

Year 2003- my employer, Quorum, held a company Christmas party in Playa Del Carmen, Mexico for employees and spouses. There were ten of us. Pale bodies lined up on beach chairs, sunscreen aroma filled the air, aquamarine waves crashed on the gleaming white sand, and we exercised our arms running the drink flag up and down the pole.

Sandra read the weekend listing of resort events out loud. She paused and with a sidelong glance at me said, "Oh look, we could all ride horses on the beach at two."

She thinks she's so funny. I gave her my maybe-I-can forget-to generate-your paycheck-look, let a final drop of Corona hit my tongue, and ran the flag up once more. This swim-suited butt was staying in its lounger for the afternoon.

Chapter 9: Future Guard Dog for Hell: Roseanne

Animals were in Ray's blood. Pre-veterinarian program in college, he worked in a vet's office and spent one summer training junkyard dogs. His family had pets for years and his parents currently own a mutt named Taz. Grandparents coddled Buster, Misty, Bart, and Sam. With his second wife, Ray went the dog show route. This was fortunate for me because he got "burned out". So, when I said I wasn't keen on creatures and would never entertain the thought of a canine in our house, Ray agreed to my marriage terms and conditions. Oh, I'm sure he thought I'd change. However, I never wavered and despite his sons' pleas, a pet never has been a member of our immediate family.

Instead the dog I heard about most and the one the boys remember was Cuno. I have to keep from saying "Cujo." From pictures, Cuno was a magnificent Great White Pyrenees. Ray claimed the dog, taller than the toddlers, kept an eye on the boys when they played outside and was a good babysitter. Ray always says, "If you have to bend over to pet it, it's not a dog." No small yappy creatures for Ray or the boys. Think big. Me, I'd rather opt for daycare. Plus I'm glad I don't sweep up dog hair.

Lucky for me, I could visit Ray's family and their dogs, hear tales of Red, Bill, Coco, Lefty, and Ralph from the past, and look at their pictures. There was no escape. Of course, I heard tales of Roseanne, the bitch at Pat and James' place. Her name was mentioned in hushed tones, folks made the sign of the cross for this devil incarnate. No doubt, we'd cross paths someday.

Buster was the standard bearer. He belonged to Ray's grandparents when Ray was a boy and from what I gather ran the household. No other dog since has lived up to Buster's skills. A few have been clever enough to bark and alert his grandparents to water moccasins on the porch. Useful for country living. A few have also, sadly, not been smart enough to keep from being run over. Chasing trucks is deadly sport.

Anytime we'd visit the country, dogs heralded our arrival with a lot of barking, leaping, and panting. Before car doors could open, they'd clamor to greet us. I'd fuss with my seatbelt, gather my purse, and stall until the boys diverted the dogs; or Ray's folks had the dogs under control. Then I'd open my car door and attempt to remain invisible. But, that was impossible. Dogs bounded over to greet, jump, and follow me to the house. Curious noses, hot breath, drool, muddy paws. It was always a dance for me, to maneuver away from teeth.

Ray and I weren't married yet. We were expected at his grandparents for lunch, and encountered minimal traffic on our Sunday morning drive. It was the boys' weekend at Ray's ex, so we had a peaceful ride. No yammering in the back, no "he touched me," and no wrestling. We reveled in the quiet.

Ray popped up, "You've never seen Pat and James' house, have you?"

"No, I only heard it was round."

"Hey, we'll stop by. I'm sure they haven't headed to grandmother's yet."

They lived in Kaufman near Ray's grandparents and folks. So, we took the long way to see their place. Amidst the log homes, the small ranch style buildings, the lean-to barns, and prairie style architecture, a modern round house sat like a space station on a field. "Wow. I can't wait to see inside."

Ray nodded; we pulled into the driveway, and could hear a baying type of bark. Around the corner loped a long, lean black Doberman, ears pointed, teeth bared. It howled, hackles up, lean body poised for attack.

"Roll up your window," said Ray. Hell, I'd rolled up the window and hunkered down for the onslaught. Did I see froth? Where was the holy water to splash in the dog's direction?

"That's Roseanne." He stopped the car but made no move to open his door. "We wait for James or Pat."

Silence, except for the insane barking and uproar created by this one dog. Crazy eyes, check.

55

Frantic movements, check. She didn't throw herself at the car, but she would crouch and leap depending on our movements. Would she chomp a side mirror? Erratic, scary power with sharp teeth. Then an added bonus arrived, a chow named Sarge, Roseanne's sidekick. Another berserk canine headed our way. I whimpered and ducked, the pale hairs on my arms stood up. Ray never put his hand on the car handle. We were not exiting the vehicle.

"Has the dog always been schizoid?" I asked.

"They got her as a puppy and there was always something a little off. I don't think she ever bit Pat or James, and obviously she's a good watchdog. But no one except maybe granddaddy is alone in Roseanne's presence."

Ray honked the horn, but there was no sign of life in the windows or at the front door. "Truck's gone. They must be at grandmother's early or running errands.

"Shoot, maybe Roseanne devoured them." I joked.

"Did I ever tell you the fishing story?" Ray asked and I shook my head. "I was fifteen and spending the weekend at grandmother and granddaddy's. James was over, with Roseanne in tow, so we all went to the tank. The guys spent the morning together - James, granddaddy, dogs, Roseanne, and me. Good time, plenty of fish. James and Granddaddy walked up to the house to make sandwiches. I was casting, reached over to get more bait, and Roseanne let loose with a growl. She looked at me as if she'd never seen me before. Teeth bared, throaty bark, menacing glare. I didn't

56

move until James came back. He got her settled down, but man, it was horrifying. I really thought she'd attack my arm. Ever since, I've given her a wide berth. She's mental."

I contemplated the satanic creature howling in front of us. She didn't let up. "And you wonder why I'm afraid of dogs? I'll have nightmares tonight."

Roseanne's barking registered deeper and deeper, even as we backed out the driveway. She maintained her distance but shook in her frenzy. Her prey left, no blood taken, no car parts eaten. I had seen the bodyguard for the gates of hell and I shivered.

Chapter 10: San Saba Snakes or Far From a Mall

My poor shiny black Pontiac is engulfed in white caliche dust as Ray and I bump our way to his aunt's home in San Saba. A splendid fall Saturday and we are making good time. Three hours on paved roads that went from highway to two-lane blacktop, and now we've turned off from civilization to jounce thirty minutes along a gravel dirt trail. I won't dignify it as a road. Ray's Corvette is too low slung for this adventure, so my Pontiac's shocks get a workout.

We stop at times to view some deer that pause and then leap a fence to bound away. A cow meanders across the road, though how it got past the cattle guard rails is a good question. Some turkey skitters beside us, confused as to whether to cross or not. Far from a mall or a movie theater, San Saba is hill country. Rocks and cactus dot the rugged landscape and pickup trucks rule the territory. An old Dodge Ram blows by us with the driver giving a friendly wave. I'm thrilled at the sound of pebbles plinking against my car paint.

At last we arrive at her gate. Common courtesy says I, the passenger, should get out to open the gate, let Ray drive through, close the gate, and return to the car. However, a large bull, at least I think it's a bull it looks so mean, eyes me from within charging distance. "No way am I getting out of this car," I declare.

Ray doesn't say a thing. He does roll his eyes, puts the car in park, and gets out to open the gate. He hops back in, pulls the car forward, and then repeats the process to close the gate behind us. The bull hasn't moved.

In the last hundred yards to the house, Pat's dogs tear out and run alongside the car. Uh-oh, the circus begins. The Great Pyrenees gives one deep throaty bark. Kelli's huge and could swat my car like a fly. Nick, the mutt scrapper, is all muscle, wiggle, and bark. He's happy to see us, but is scary in his enthusiasm. I wait for Pat to corral him before exiting the car. We hug as Nick scampers underfoot, tries to lick my hand and encourage me to pet him. Not going to happen. Company's here and Nick must make his mark. He circles and pees on all four of my tires. Sunday we get my car washed before it goes back into our garage.

Ray and Pat are close in age, even though she's his aunt. He volunteers to come down and help on chores and I tag-a-long. She manages this property herself now that her husband, James, is gone, and 225 acres is a lot of land, even though the majority is undeveloped. James retired quite early and the goal was to hunt, fish, and build a house. Rock by rock, they chiseled their way through to create a comfortable small ranch home. Cozy two-bedroom, the highlight is the breathtaking view from any window. Pinks, oranges, and purples color some sunsets. Banks of storm clouds develop in the distance and roll through the hills. Coyotes bay at the moon, and as always deer appear, in silhouetted morning fog, only to fade away like eerie ghosts. James haunted by Vietnam flashbacks, lost his spirit and passed far too young.

Anyway, we unload our overnight bags and Pat offers glasses of lemonade. She kindly keeps the dogs outside, in my honor, and Kelli and Nick both stand at the front door in disbelief. Noses pressed against the screen, mournful eyes stare, and an occasional bark from Nick is designed to remind Pat that she couldn't possibly have meant to close the door in his face. Kelli gives up and plops down smack dab in front of the door. Fine, if she can't come in, then they won't be able to get out. She's a smart girl. Nick is relentless. He runs to the back, in case maybe Pat will let him in there. He strains to peer into the dining room; he might be missing out on a snack. Then, he tears back to the front door, ever hopeful that something has changed in the last thirty seconds.

Ray asks Pat, "Shall we tour the place in the Jeep and take care of the flagpole problem."

"Excellent. Did y'all bring boots? The snakes are on the move before they settle into hibernation."

Snakes?! I knew to bring my boots, but I hate hearing that the snakes are in slither mode. That makes hiking very difficult. I'll have to watch my step and ignore scenic views.

We pile into the Jeep and that includes Nick, proud to be in the backseat with Pat. Panting with excitement, he can't contain himself. He wants to hang his head out my window flap and his hot breath makes me conscious of his teeth. When he swings his head back inside, a big pile of drool splats on my headrest. Pat daubs it with a greasy rag. Nick hovers closer to me. Pat pulls him back, but he is more determined. I lean to the left, nearer to Ray and away we go on the rather unformed paths left by hunters who rent the deer lease.

Tall grasses, brambly mesquite shrub, and cactus are our path. Ray swerves to avoid jagged boulders, and our heads bounce against the Jeep headliner. Kelli runs alongside us and detours to lap some water or even take a dip in a mud hole. Ray stops the Jeep briefly to negotiate a large gouge in the road. Pat yells at her, "No, do not shake dry near us," and Kelli actually listens. Her pure white coat is now a coffee brown and the long fur entraps burrs. Like a youngster who dug in the dirt all day, Kelli needs a bath.

Ray has hunted here with James, and he re-lives various deer or wild pig episodes with stories. Like the fish that got away, the deer point numbers grow exponentially. Now the only deer I've seen here look like big dogs. But there's always the mythic buck, Big Boy as James called him, which roams the hillside. Or the meanest hog stared them

61

down, red squinty eyes and foot long tusks. Beers and lies. Isn't that what hunting is all about?

We drive slowly to look at feeders and stands. Pat points, "There's a new stand. James would have laughed at the placement. It's too open." Rental is most of her income and livelihood. At times we get out of the Jeep to walk to an area. I'm careful to stay on the path, to watch for snakes, and also avoid huge stinky cow patties. Nature is messy. I think I smell a skunk or something noxious. Pat pulls out a pistol and I'm ducking for cover while looking and listening for a rattler. "Joanne, there's nothing here. I need Ray to test the sights. I found this gun when I cleaned the shed and I need to know if it is in good working order." She hands the pistol to Ray who proceeds to examine the barrel, loads a bullet, releases the safety, and aims for a target that a hunter left in this hollow. I fear the bullet will ricochet off a rock, and I nervously pace.

"Stop moving, so I can fire." Ray says through clenched teeth. I halt, he shoots, and I flinch from the reverberation. The pistol fire echoes through the hills and for a brief second, I'm conscious that the hum of birds silences. Ray walks to view the target, and outdoor sounds resume. Birds chatter. A cow bellows in the distance and Nick barks at something. Nodding, Ray's happy with the pistol and returns it to Pat. "You might want to clean it up some more, but it's in good shape for snake shooting." Pat doesn't hunt, but she does not put up with snakes on her front porch. The dogs inform her of an intruder and she fires first and asks questions later. Even the thought of it puts me in a swoon.

Back into the Jeep for the final run up the largest hill to the flagpole, something stinks and it's not me, nor is it Pat or Ray. Hot, sweaty, doggy Nick reeks. Pat pushes him out of the vehicle, despite his protests, and we exhale. It takes awhile for the wind whistling through the open windows to clear the odor. A faint smell of smoke is welcome, and we're glad a neighbor is burning trash. The last fifteen minutes of the ride is wicked to my untrained eye. Looks like we could tumble off the precipice with another gust of wind. Ray's an excellent driver, but even he grips the Jeep wheel with both hands and concentrates. Chu-chug and we grind to a halt. Nick and Kelli swarm the car. I'm never ready for their pushy noses and desire to be near us. I keep my hands close to my body and turn to get tools from the car. Though we are in an unmowed area I assume the dogs would act crazy if a snake was on the move. I step confidently from my seat.

This is the James memorial, the highest point of his land and of San Saba County and the view is amazing, in that John Ford western way. Raw land. No signs, minimal barbed wire fencing, no cut up cubicles of yards with sprinkler systems. Cue the music and pan the camera. Look for clouds of dust in the distance heralding the arrival of a stagecoach. Or imagine Indian braves on bareback. This land teems with insects, furry creatures, cattle, wild horses, deer, and barely cedes accommodation for man. It is unforgiving and majestic. I'm grateful to

63

visit, but I couldn't live here. The vast distances of blue-sky nothingness also means there are no conveniences. I am too far from access to creature comforts.

Back from my reverie, Pat explains our mission. "We need to get down the tattered flag and put up a new one. I have to do it quarterly since the wind is so destructive. James' brother, Tim, fixed up the wire cord and rope to not fray and snap. Now it is almost too foolproof. You have to jiggle that part there to slowly lower the flag." She demonstrated the technique. This was going to take awhile and it was not a one-person show. Ray started angling, flicking one side of the cord and then the other. Pat helped maneuver another piece. I stood behind Ray and helped brace him. He'd been having some vertigo problems and standing there looking straight up was dizzying. From our spot on this hill, the tall flagpole, and the ever-whipping wind, this was time consuming. Between the three of us, we got the new flag unfurled and flying high. Gasping a bit from the exertion and strain, we rubbed our necks and reflected on ornery, fun-loving, wild man, James. He'd have climbed the pole and had the job done in minutes. Foul-mouthed, fearless, and athletic, James fit this land and vice versa. He could be a little boy at play, or a no-nonsense man defending his territory. Now, he had the best seat to survey his domain and keep watch over Pat.

Something snapped and I jumped, looking for a snake or a creature. Nick appeared, ready to hitch a ride. Still stinky, he was denied passage. Ray, Pat, and I hopped aboard the Jeep for a descent back into her valley. We'd worked up an appetite for a fresh fish fry.

Sated from our fried fish, fried tater tots, and fried onion rings, we sit on Pat's porch in the darkness, watch and listen. I'm accustomed to a constant nightglow from streetlights and the sheer blackness is unnerving and yet invigorating. Ray takes my arm and we step out to look up into the sky. Crisp and clear, the stars sparkle and wink. An owl hoots. Insects creak and buzz. There's a rustle. Could be the cows or the horses. Even domesticated Kelli roams freely. Pat says, "I could rebuild a cow or a deer with the bones that Kelli retrieves and brings to me. She is pleased with her offerings and so proud, like a kid with a shell from the beach." My face must have reflected horror or disgust because Pat continued, "It is gross at times."

I admire her matter-of-fact attitude and her pioneer spirit. She deals with feed and hay and taking cows to sell at market. She witnesses the birth of a colt from one of the mares, afterbirth left on the trail. Blood and guts and raw nature. Daily miracles that I would prefer to not see live, but rather through the sterile lens of a National Geographic television special. I'm a city girl. How or why did I end up in this family and with Ray?

Sunday morning and after a heaping country breakfast of eggs, sausage, and biscuits we decide to walk before we head back to Bedford. Sweatshirt weather, and of course, boots. Dogs bound alongside us. Nick stops to pee on my tires again perhaps as a talisman so we won't leave. He's barked at me less and seems resigned to being outdoors full-time during our visit. I stumble over a rock on the path and nearly careen into cactus. I look for snakes, cow droppings, and pretty much anything ground level. Uncoordinated, I have trouble walking a straight line under pure road conditions. This rough terrain is not for a tenderfoot. Less windy today, but we look to the hill and the new flag waves, its red, white, and blue glorious against the pale hued early morning sky.

Though you can't see Pat's neighbors, aromas suggest a bacon sizzling Sunday morning. A shot rings out from far away. Target practice in preparation for deer season. As we round a corner on our path, there stand some deer. Not skittish yet. Fat and happy, they continue to nibble on some leaves. Then with a quick flicker of a tail, they turn and leap away. So fast and so smooth, they blend into the brush and evaporate. Further up the trail, a rabbit scoots by and startles us all.

Our nature walk a success, Ray and I round up our bags and prepare to leave. Pat thinks of one final plumbing question. With tools in hand, Ray heads to this project. I load the car and then hover in the front yard area. Kick a stone, bend down to look at a flower; I wander around admiring Pat's

66

plant pots and hummingbird feeders. A few minutes later, leaning against Pat's beat-up pickup truck, I realize I am surrounded. Both dogs scamper near me. Kelli blocks my path. Three cows have decided to graze within yards of me. And the skittish horses are right behind the truck. They neigh and shake their manes. Well fed by Pat, but too wild to saddle up and ride, the horses are unpredictable. The baby colt teeters on skinny legs next to the mare. His white blaze stands out on his narrow face. I look around. No sudden movements. The cows step closer. No, there's not enough grass here, go yonder down the path. I silently beg for Ray to fix the leak and hurry out here. I don't know what the horses are doing. One bumps the back end of the truck. He might have been scratching himself. I play statue and stand in my safe spot, not on a fire ant hill, not in the middle of some poo.

"Smile. Look like you're having fun." Ray snaps a picture and Pat laughs. The dogs break for her and she shoos the cows away from her yard.

"You should have seen your face," Ray chuckles. With that I realize my role. I'm the court jester, the entertainment, and the Yankee girl in the Texas Faries show. Ray's my snake wrangler and charmer all rolled into one.

Chapter 11: Who Was That Masked Turtle?

Boys and creeks equaled frogs, snakes, and turtles. No matter how much of a concrete jungle surrounded us, boys discovered running water and managed to arrive home sopping wet, muddy, and with squishy sneakers that oozed goo for weeks. If I caught them in time, like border control, I'd halt garage door entry. A search ensued. "You vill empty all zee pockets, you vill remove zee mucky clothes, you vill not touch anyzing." (Yes, I spoke in a German accent. It sounded so much scarier than my Spanish Inquisition impression.)

My efforts, for the most part, were fruitless. A lot happened in the time between their end of school day and my home from work time. I counted on my keen sense of animal awareness and their inability at subterfuge to stave off too many surprises. They did get better at wiping up huge puddles. I know frogs lived in jars (with air holes) under beds. Fortunately, Ray was more apt to banish creek entertainment than me. He was extremely pissed when the boys wanted to measure the distance for phone coverage and dropped our mobile into the creek.

"Why is the phone dripping water?"

"I don't know."

"Where did you take the phone?"

"Maybe to the creek..."

Both Chris and Kevin were grounded for life from the phone and the creek for that escapade. That was a torturous week for us with bored, caged kids, but Ray never wavered. It also took forever for allowance money to pay for a new phone.

One lazy summer Saturday, Ray and I floated in the pool, neglecting the yard, chores, and even the boys. They'd turn up sooner or later. It was almost lunchtime. Sure enough, the door banged and out came seven-year old Kevin, tanned and barefoot. Even with his head shorn for the summer, his cowlick stuck up. Following him was nine-year old, sunburned Chris. He'd inherited his father's freckle face, yet loathed slathering on sunscreen. He carried something and Kevin danced around him with excitement. Without my glasses, I'm blind. Thus, from my float, I squinted but could not tell what they had.

"Hey," Kevin squealed. "Look at our turtle. Can we keep him? I know he wants to live with us."

"Not in the house," I said, immediately squelching the summer fun. Ray and I floundered up the pool steps to dry off. I donned my glasses and got a good look at the box turtle being handed back and forth like a beach ball. Its head tucked, the turtle, no doubt, feared for its life.

Ray appealed to common sense. "I'm sure he's not happy being away from his home and family. He belongs back in the creek."

"Oh no. He walked right to us," Kevin said. Chris nodded in agreement and added, "It can be a science project. We'll read up and study Tank. That's his name." Chris was clever to appeal to the educational aspect, but I wasn't falling for Mr. Science this time.

Meanwhile, Kevin frowned. "No, I said his name was Torpedo."

"That's stupid."

"Well, I saw him first." They bickered while the turtle fried on the deck. Ray grabbed the hose and sprayed some water on Tank/Torpedo.

"Boys, you can have the turtle as a visitor right now. But you must return him to the creek this afternoon....no arguments." Ray ignored their protest. "It's cruel to keep him here in a box or whatever you plan. He can't be in the pool because it has chlorine. The creek...I mean it."

Whew! I hadn't had to say a word. Ray was the party pooper on this episode.

"Can we get the old plastic tub for him right now?" Kevin called from the shed.

"That's fine. Get your turtle situated; then, wash your hands for lunch. Hurry up." I decided to make grilled cheese sandwiches. Tank/Torpedo wouldn't hurt anything on the patio. He poked his head out once and ducked back immediately. I figured the boys would tire quickly of the lack of excitement.

70

Word spread and Matt, Justin, Russ, and other neighbor kids trooped to the deck to visit the turtle. Proud as punch, the boys poked, prodded, and played with their prized possession. I'm surprised they didn't charge admission. The turtle gamely survived the activities. Perhaps this was an adventure for him. It was a slow day in Bedford. Ray hung around to watch baseball on TV and I escaped the heat with a movie matinee. I arrived back home around five to find Ray in the kitchen seasoning burgers to grill.

He gave me a kiss. "The boys and their entourage left with Tank/Torpedo for the creek. As soon as they come back, I'll fire up dinner."

"That worked out well. I'm glad I didn't have to speak."

"Yep. Hell, I felt sorry for the damn thing," Ray said. I nodded in agreement.

Summer rolled along and every so often, the boys showed up with Tank in tow. (Chris won the name game.) They'd haul out the plastic tub and watch the turtle scramble to get out. He'd slip and slide and sooner or later give up his attempt to escape. I have to say he was a harmless diversion. Within an hour of his arrival, I'd hear the door bang. "Joanne, come see Tank. He knows us and when we call his name he peeks out. Can't we keep him here?" Kevin would bat those long dark lashes and plead.

Ogre that I am, I'd shake my head. "Nope. He can visit, but belongs in his creek. Not gonna change my mind." I'd resume reading my paper, but out of the corner of my eye, I'd see the shoulders slump. Kevin would mumble under his breath and shuffle back outside. So distraught. So put-upon. Once in awhile, I'd almost break. I'd question myself, but then the thoughts of salmonella or other turtle spread diseases came to mind and I'd vow to remain firm.

At the end of the day, Chris or Kevin or both would haul the turtle back to the creek bed.

Back to school late August and less time for creek adventures. Both boys began soccer and that's a lifetime commitment between practice and games. So, sports and school filled our lives. Days shortened, temperatures cooled, and soon it was Halloween. It was a good year for vampires and monsters. We had the house decorated with fake spider webs and pumpkins. Scary haunted house music blasted from speakers and tons of kids roamed the streets for candy.

Then it was time to clear the way for end-of-year holidays. A week after Halloween, I was in Chris's room to vacuum and put away laundry. I opened his closet and decided to neaten the piles of toys and football gear. Something shifted and out tumbled his wadded up black vampire cape. I grabbed an end and gave it a shake. Thunk, Tank landed on the carpet, rolled once, and wobbled. I screamed and stepped back. He was between the door and me. I stood paralyzed. Oh my God, was the turtle alive?_ I leaned over, but saw no sign of movement.

Footsteps. Ray stormed into the room, concern on his face. "What happened? I heard your scream from the garage." Chris and Kevin followed him in. I pointed to the floor.

"What the...? Is that...?" Ray was flabbergasted.

"Yes, he rolled out of this cape. He's been smothered in plastic in the closet. Aack, I might be sick. Is he dead?"

"Chris, what were you thinking? You might have killed him." Ray shouted. Both boys snuffled and looked scared.

"We thought he'd be cold. But I forgot I had him in there," said Chris. "Dad what are you going to do?"

Ray stood over the turtle. Leery, he grabbed a hockey stick and prodded it. Nothing. Then, a tiny flurry of leg activity. "I think he's alive." Ray reached down and turned Tank over. "Dehydrated, for sure. I'm going to put some water in the plastic tub and bring him out to the patio." Ray moved to the door.

"Wait, don't leave me here."

"Well, do you want to get the tub?" I nodded and tiptoed around the hard-shelled creature lying comatose on the floor.

I exhaled, ran to the shed, got the tub, and splashed some water into it. Ray came outside holding Tank by its shell. The boys shadowed him. "He's wiggled his legs. No head yet. We'll see what happens."

"The water's brisk," I said.

"Shouldn't matter. Turtles are cold-blooded creatures." Ray placed the turtle into the tub and stepped back. As we held our breaths, out poked a head. Slowly, Tank walked a few steps, blinked, and stopped. The boys clapped and vowed they'd return him to his creek home without a roundtrip ticket. Ray was glad he didn't have to do mouth-to-mouth resuscitation.

Turtles are hardy creatures, but I'd say a few more days and we were close to turtle soup.

In the future, I avoided boys' closets.

Chapter 12: Is That Chirping I Hear?

How many times can one hear "please, please, please, please"? It took a lot, but I succumbed to Kevin's pleas. Those deep brown eyes with long eyelashes yearned like a Dickens urchin. The impish grin and dimpled cheeks projected unchecked hope. Kevin, age eleven, was a good kid and he loved animals. A huge pet store opened near us and he rode his bike there every day after school. Not old enough to hold a job, he offered his free labor, and came home with stories of hugging puppies and balancing birds, cleaning cages, sweeping floors, and charming customers. I'd listen but say, "Kevin, wash your hands. Lord knows what you've touched." Sometimes he smelled like pee.

Kevin persuaded Ray and me to visit the store with him. Pet-O-Rama was huge and I was taken aback by the noise. A cacophony of customer laughter, animal yaps, squeals, bird whistles, and even a quack assaulted my ears. Kids ran amok and parents followed with baskets of feed, cages, and assorted pet gear. There was an underlying scent of Pine sol covering urine, sweat, and something that stank like gym socks. Workers swept the floor and had towels ready for accidents. I dodged a puddle of mystery fluid.

Introducing us to every animal, Kevin showed us his favorites, and like a puppy wagging his tail he begged for attention. Not heartless, I peered into cages and admired the beauty of some bird's coloring. I conceded the cuteness value of puppies and kittens, but I dismissed any hints to purchase or offer a home to said animals. No petting or cooing on my part. Hands stayed in my pockets and I kept my distance from anything with a licking tongue.

Clever, Kevin deduced that I wasn't falling for his interactive presentation. He had a backup plan and maneuvered us towards the fish aisle. Tanks gurgled and the colorful array of tropical treasures swirled through clear waters. His fingers entwined, feet shuffling, Kevin gave it his all, "Please, can I have a small tank and two Betas?" He pointed towards brilliant blue fish with lacy fins. I wavered and he went in for the kill. "I'll clean the tank, and you don't have to see them except in my room, and they don't run around, and…."

I had actually thought fish could be a possible solution to the 'evil stepmother won't let me have a pet' problem. Thus, I put my hand up and said one fateful word, "Yes."

Ray's head spun toward me, eyebrows raised, mouth open in astonishment. I nodded that I meant what I'd said.

Meanwhile, Kevin prattled on, " ...I'll use my allowance money. I've been saving up, and ..." He stopped. My answer filtered through his brain and registered. If a kid could leap and touch the clouds, that was the scene. Ray and I witnessed his absolute excitement, joy, and sheer enthusiasm. Despite my misgivings, I was happy with his reaction, and he was thrilled he'd finally have a pet.

Tank, filter, two Betas – one blue, one yellow, fish food, aquarium stones, and my pick – a pirate's treasure chest for atmosphere. Pets are expensive. Crestfallen at the register, the kid saw his dream fade as the clerk tallied the fish project. Heroic, Ray subsidized the project when handfuls of crumpled ones didn't cover the tab.

Proud of his conquest, Kevin cradled the bags of fish on the ride home. He talked to them, "We're on Harwood, now we turn, and there's our house." He leaped from the car to run show Chris. Books and paper were swept off Kevin's nightstand to make way for the tank. I left Ray to read instructions and help with set up. I'd done my part. Now it was up to the kid to keep the fish alive.

Sunday morning, I read the paper, Ray showered, and Chris was still in bed. (Yes, he slept a lot to avoid life, his annoying younger brother, and us.) Kevin, normally a perky morning person, wandered into the kitchen and plopped into a chair. He looked disheartened. "Hey, g'morning. What's up?" I asked, lowering the comics to observe.

"I think Smurf killed Stinger last night."

It took me a moment to realize we weren't discussing some computer game characters. This was real life.

"I assume Stinger was the yellow one? I thought they were getting along. Do you need to bury him?"

Kevin was disconsolate. "Yeah. I thought I had a male and a female. They'd be okay. But I guess I got two males and Beta males fight. I know that happened to Matt's fish. Stinger was like half-eaten. I scooped him out and flushed."

That was not an image I needed so I went back to my paper. "You've got Smurf. He can rule the tank. There's waffles in the freezer for breakfast."

He sighed and dragged himself back to his room. I guess I didn't give enough sympathy. I informed Ray of the death in the family, and he went to see to Kevin. Back in the kitchen to cook some eggs, Ray said, "That's fish life. He's going to save and probably buy a new Beta next week. The cycle will go on. He'll learn."

Sure enough, fish came and went quickly. Beta wars, overeating, starvation, and water chemical problems were only a few of the issues surrounding Kevin's tank. He did attend to it, so I never regretted my decision. When I went into his room to drop off laundry, I'd tap on the glass and watch colorful Betas scurry about seeking food. After a year or so, the fish fling ended and the tank sat empty. I was in the clear.

"Do I hear a chirp? What's in that bag?" Home from work early, I was in the kitchen preparing spaghetti for dinner. Entering from the garage, Kevin and Matt walked through the kitchen, mumbled a hello, and sped up. They looked guilty.

"We're going to my room." Nonchalant, Kevin eased the bag into Matt's hands. I was on full radar alert, gave another stir to the ground beef, added tomato sauce, and lowered the burner heat.

"What's in the bag?" I asked again. I knew that I wasn't going to want to know what was in the bag, but darn it, they forced me to pursue the answer. Why couldn't they be sneakier? Crap, why couldn't they go to Matt's house with suspicious items?

Kevin succumbed to my glare. "Crickets."

"Live crickets? Why?"

"Um," his voice cracked, "for my lizard."

Oh good Lord._ An image of a Gila monster flashed into my brain. Goose bumps raised on my arms. "You have a lizard? Who said you could have a lizard?" My voice screeched. "Does your father know about lizards? We're going to talk about this."

I went back to vigorous stirring. The two hovered and then slunk out of the room. I could hear Matt in the living room. "Dude, you are so busted." Kevin responded but I couldn't hear. Matt didn't stay long and he left by the front door. Guess he couldn't face the wrath of Joanne.

Ray arrived from work, oblivious to our new family crisis. He kissed me and asked, "How was your day? Man, traffic was a pain. Smells good."

"Chris is at football. He'll be home later. Call Kevin to the table now." I splatted spaghetti portions on three plates.

"Okay..." Ray hesitated, started to ask me a question, thought better of it, and called Kevin to the table. Ray knew he'd learn the situation soon enough. He was right in guessing that the "problem" was his son who yanked open the fridge to pour some milk and sunk down in his chair without his usual cheery, "Hey Dad."

Silent, we shook Parmesan cheese on our spaghetti, passed the garlic bread, and slurped our noodles. Kevin got up to pour more milk. As he sat down, I watched him flick his hair out of his eyes, frown, and give a sidelong look towards his father. His face flickered with emotion and I knew I could count on him to break first.

"Dad, I've got two lizards in my tank and they are really cool. I got 'em from a guy at school. It's no big deal. They eat crickets and drink water. I already had the tank and they're not going to get any bigger or escape or nothin'. Joanne's freaking out about the crickets."

I chimed in then, "Well yeah. We spray to keep bugs out of our house and here he's bringing in crickets. And he has lizards; I'm not keen on that…"

"He didn't ask. He just did it," I added.

Ray kept eating and with a mouthful of bread asked, "How long have you had the lizards?"

Kevin looked at me and answered his dad. "Two weeks. See they don't do a thing."

Ray glanced at me and then returned to his plate. "He's got a point. You haven't noticed the lizards."

I pursed my lips. "I don't go into his room now that he's in charge of cleaning it. But, I don't care. He should have asked about lizards. I allowed fish. But lizards...scales, flicking tongues, webbed feet, slithering up walls...that's creepy."

"Let me see them." Ray wiped his mouth with his napkin and indicated that Kevin should lead the way. He slouched ahead of his father. I finished my meal and started to clear the table. The duo returned. Kevin saw his plate was gone. "I'm going to do homework in my room," he said and left the kitchen.

Ray put butter back in the fridge. "It's two little brownish greenish lizards and there's a lid on the tank with air holes. I don't see that it's going to hurt anything. I told him to keep it clean and he can't let the crickets loose. Plus they are more likely to stink than the lizards."

"Oh great," I said.

"I know you are annoyed, but it'll be fine. I told Kevin that if you found crickets wandering the house, everything had to go. He understands," Ray gave me a half-hug.

I did not smile and give in that easily. I'll probably have a lizard dream tonight. Serve you right if I wake up screaming, pointing at the ceiling. "We'll see," I said shutting the dishwasher and turning its dials. The discussion ended with the uproar of churning water.

Kept my eyes peeled for crickets, but I was not surprised by an invasion at that end of the house. I avoided Kevin's room and should learn to not come home early from work. One day, Kevin had the television up loud so he must not have heard my arrival. I rounded the corner of the family room and he was sitting in the chair with a lizard on his arm. The tongue flicked, eyes unblinking. Taken aback, I pointed, waved, and flapped my lips. Kevin took the hint, sighed, and returned the lizard to its tank. I didn't dare think about lizards crawling on the leather sofa where I sit.

A few months went by. Ray and I were in the backyard trimming bushes. Kevin came outside to make an announcement. "You'll be happy to know that I gave the lizards to Matt. They're gone."

"Good. Thank you. What caused this?" I asked.

"I'll admit the crickets were a little gross and if the lizards killed them but didn't eat them right away, they kinda stank. I was tired of 'em, and Matt said he'd take them, so it all works out. I'm going to Matt's now and then we might go swimming at Russ's. See ya."

"Problem solved," said Ray. He stopped trimming and turned towards me. "I'm so brilliant. I knew the lizards wouldn't last too long."

"Don't hurt your arm patting yourself on the back. That's it for creatures. I've done my part, no longer the evil stepmother. I surrendered to a twinge of guilt and it got me fish and lizards. I survived it, but do you know how much I've suffered?"

"No. But, I'm thinking it's time for a dog." Ray ducked.

Chapter 13: The Guinea Pig Surrenders

May 1996 was my lost month. I lost my mind, my judgment, and any semblance of control. The school year almost over, my husband, Ray, and I hoped Chris, newly sixteen, found a job for the summer. However his plans sounded like that of a vampire – sleep by day, roam at night. Amazingly enough, employers didn't knock on our front door and beg to hire Chris. As far as I knew he had yet to fill out an application. To assuage my nagging, he brought home forms, but then they didn't move from the kitchen counter. I enlisted Ray to forward the job plan.

Kevin, at fourteen, was industrious. He helped at the nearby pet store, mowed some lawns, and had plenty of friends. With the go-kart in pieces, he had a project and goal of re-assembly and speed. One afternoon in the garage, Kevin, Matt, and Justin rummaged through Ray's bolt collection. Out front to pull weeds, I could hear their conversation.

Matt, tall and gangly, said, "You know I leave next week for my Dad's in Colorado."

"For how long?" Kevin asked.

"A month. It's cool. Dad said he bought me a new mountain bike and we'd go up to Durango." His dad was a heart surgeon, so Matt was the rich kid out of this crew. He always had the latest gadgets.

Justin mumbled something about borrowing Matt's old bike here while he was gone. I think I heard a yes. Then I overheard a fateful sentence from Matt.

"My Mom said I needed to find someone to watch Twinkle for the month. She and my stepdad are traveling and won't be home to feed her or give water."

"Huh, maybe I can do it somehow. Would your Mom give me a key and I could come to your house?" Kevin asked.

"Nah. Ever since Ryan screwed up something while we were gone, she's berserk over setting the alarm and stuff," Matt replied. I remembered that story. I liked Matt's stepbrother, but he was trouble and pretty much banished from this neighborhood. I stayed in my spot and yanked every weed possible. I could hear the kids bang tool drawers, the clank of metal.

"I'll ask my Dad. I bet I can get Twinkle since it's only a month," said Kevin. "Here's what we need for the wheel. Let's go."

I had time to scoot to the middle of the yard as they trooped out of the garage and back to the vehicular carcass. Weeds in hand, I mulled over my strategy. Twinkle was a guinea pig and no way was I going to allow such a creature into my house. Kevin had owned fish and two lizards. That was enough. He'd graduate in a few years. Then he could go on his own and have as many animals as he wanted.

Kevin used Ray's power to convince me that I'd never know Twinkle was in the house. I must have acquiesced while under the influence of tequila. Ray knew when to concoct his killer margaritas and enchiladas. He felt sorry for Matt and Kevin and took their side. My powers diminished, I weakened and agreed. Ray, Chris, Kevin, and Matt outnumbered me. As the transfer occurred, all swore the month would zoom by with nary a mess. Kevin had a cage, food, and Twinkle (what a silly name for a rodent). She sniffed the air. Kevin poked his finger into her cage. "Aren't you the best girl?" he said. She promptly bit him. He drew back and sucked on his pinkie. "Feisty. I like that," he grinned. I didn't appreciate seeing sharp little teeth. Nonetheless, I wouldn't enter Kevin's room and Twinkle could spin on her wheel and enjoy his hospitality. I was such a fool.

I reminded Kevin of the lizard on the couch incident. "Oh, Twinkle will only be out of her cage when I clean it. She'll be in my room and I swear not in the living room." Lots of swearing in this household, you'd think they were Boy Scouts. So, we waved goodbye to Matt and assured him we'd keep Twinkle alive. I crossed my arms as Kevin shut his bedroom door, and once again Ray gave me his charmer's kiss and a reassuring hug.

Two weeks in, Kevin had a postcard from Matt with a "Say hi to Twinkle" on it. "He'd better bring me a good souvenir," Kevin said. Twinkle's glow faded. Awake at night, she squealed and ran circles on her wheel. He had to refill her water bottle and she tended to flick her food between the bars. The novelty over, Kevin griped while cleaning her cage and I heard him talk to her. "You are a pig, aren't you? Yuck."

I'd smile to myself, pleased at Kevin's torture. So far, Twinkle had not bothered me.

Only one more babysitting week left for Kevin. I came home from work on a Thursday ready to take a swim. Muffled television sounds in one room, stereo blared in another, and both Chris and Kevin in the family room. Down on their knees, one peered under the couch, the other under the loveseat. Pillows askew.

"What's going on?" I asked. Both kids jumped up and turned to me.

"We were looking for something." Chris replied, eyes wide.

"For what?"

Kevin mumbled, "Twinkle."

"Speak up, what did you say you are looking for?" I heard him, but had to hear it again.

"Oh, Twinkle. She escaped. I must not have shut her cage right after I cleaned it this morning. She was there. I went for a swim. Came back in my room. And she was gone." Kevin was pale and I could see a hint of tear. He got that glassy look. Both boys awaited a blowup from me. Stupid darn Matthew and his pet. Oh, I was mad and I wanted

87

to cry. I didn't want a guinea pig running loose in my house. "Keep looking. You'd better damn well find him." I tried not to curse at or in front of them, but this was a worthy occasion. "I'm calling your father. It's his fault too." Yes, that was irrational, but I didn't care. Ray must share the blame.

I went for a swim and thrashed at my anger. That damn Twinkle better not be in my pretty room (my oasis – books, no TV, comfy chairs). Damn guinea pig better not be in my kitchen cupboards, or bathroom, or…crap. They'd better find Twinkle. Now I was concerned. Where could she be? Is she in my bed?

Towel wrapped around me, I stepped in to check progress and saw that Ray hightailed it home, changed clothes, and began the search. He looked up from his sprawl in the dining room.

"Better find Twinkle. No one is leaving here tonight until she's found. No fur ball, no fun." That's all I said. I retrieved a book and retired to the patio. My concentration lagged. I moved to the float and drifted aimlessly.

Ray came outside, and I paddled closer to where he stood at the edge of the pool. "I'm going to order pizza for dinner. We'll find Twinkle. She's probably scared by now and confused. She'll get hungry or thirsty. Don't worry."

"Pizza's fine. Call me when it's here." I pushed my raft away and closed my eyes.

It was a quiet dinner and Twinkle did not make a surprise appearance or pull up a chair. Afterwards, Chris and Kevin resumed their search.

I retreated to the bedroom to watch movie rentals but jumped at any noise, rustle, or hint of a shadow of a creature on my floor or in my bed. My imagination went wild. This wasn't good.

At least no one argued about going to a friend's house. They comprehended the enormity of the Twinkle fiasco. Ray came to bed. "It's lights out. The boys are exhausted. We figure Twinkle will be in sight in the morning due to hunger. Or she'll rustle in Kevin's room tonight. You know how much crap is in his closets. She could hide anywhere. Goodnight." We kissed. I had trouble sleeping. I listened for the whisper of little paws or a teensy squeak, and I refused to get up to go to the bathroom in the middle of the night. I was in agony by the time the alarm sounded.

Friday morning Ray and I prepared for work. I sent him out on reconnaissance. "No sign of Twinkle. Kevin's already up and looking." It was safe to eat my breakfast though I opened the cupboard carefully to grab the cereal box. As if Twinkle would have hold of it and we'd struggle for Captain Crunch. Ray and I left for work. He called me mid-afternoon. "Just got off the phone with Kevin. No sign. I told him he could take a break and swim. Poor kid. He's worried."

"You said Twinkle would show up. She'd be hungry or thirsty. Now what?"

"I don't know. I'll see ya tonight." Ray clicked off.

This went on for a week. Now we were counting the hours until Matt's return. The empty cage taunted Kevin. We had serious discussions about death and whether Twinkle was suffering. Inwardly I suffered, careful to turn on lights at night before entering a room. Cautious when opening doors, as if Twinkle was about to shout, "boo!" Kevin pursued his usual summer activities, but I saw him peer behind furniture in whatever room he was in. He's got a keen nose and assured me he sniffed around for Twinkle or pee. At this point, I believed she'd been kidnapped. There were no droppings, no chew marks. Absolutely no sign she existed.

Less than six hours until Matt's return. It was a quiet Saturday. I decided to throw in a load of laundry and then head outside for a swim. Turned on the washer, poured detergent, and crammed in coloreds. Movement. I saw something out of my right eye. I turned and there, in a slow crawl, was Twinkle. If she had a white flag, she'd have waved it. I was barefoot and stepped back. However, she barely twitched. I called out but over the sound of the washer no one could hear me. She's not going anywhere. I left the laundry room as is and rousted Kevin in his room. "Twinkle's alive."

He scrambled out of bed and rushed to the laundry room. She hadn't moved. "Oh, she's so skinny." He scooped her up in his hands and cooed. "Look at her." I shook my hands indicating he needed to get Twinkle out of my area. I think he gave her a kiss and murmured into his cupped hands. "Your daddy's coming home. You need to eat and drink. Be happy." Kevin called back to me, "I'm so glad she didn't die."

90

Yeah, me too. I'm glad I didn't have a stinky corpse in my laundry room.

Matt arrived at five. I swore he'd grown two more inches in his month away. Souvenir t-shirt in hand for Kevin, he gathered up Twinkle, her cage, and supplies. He thanked us all and walked away talking to Twinkle. "I need to fatten you up. Didn't Kevin feed you? Were you a good girl?"

We shut the front door. Kevin exhaled and said, "Close call, huh?"

"Yep," I said as I poured Ray and myself a celebratory margarita. "Also, pets- no,no,no, hell no, not ever, never, no and absolutely no."

Ray piped up, "She means it this time, Kevin." Then he had the gall to wink.

Chapter 14: There's a Pit Bull in My House

Five years after his high school graduation, Kevin completed his Marine Corp duties and was honorably discharged as a Sergeant. Left our home as a boy and was returning to Texas as a man and a husband. Married for two years to Maria, he also had a baby of sorts – a pit bull puppy named Rusty. Kevin remembered what I said, "You may have as many animals as you want once you have your own place." He's also his father's son. No little pipsqueak dogs. Instead, Kevin went full steam ahead with the scariest dog on the planet, my worst nightmare, though black Dobermans or Rottweilers run close seconds

Lots of phone calls between Kevin and Ray in the month prior to the big move. Kevin researched apartments on-line and then asked Ray to check some out in person. Mailed documents and some faxes flew between Texas and San Diego. Kevin learned a lot in the Marines including strategic planning and execution of said plans. He had money coordinated, a target move-in date, a U-Haul truck, and a job interview ready in the wings.

Memorial Weekend, 2005. Kevin called Ray, "I'm officially signed out of the Marines. Maria and I are heading east." They had a truck crammed with furniture, a puppy on board and Kevin driving like a maniac. Then, ahead of schedule, Kevin's tired voice said, "We're in Fort Worth. Be there in twenty minutes." It was a Saturday afternoon and Ray ran to the grocery store for ingredients to make his famous sour cream chicken enchiladas. I got out of the pool, cleaned up, and made sure the guest room was presentable. Moving day was set for Sunday. In an insane lapse of judgment, I volunteered that Kevin and Maria and Rusty could spend Saturday night. As I plumped pillows, I questioned myself. Why am I allowing a pit bull in my house?

Screech. Truck brakes announced their arrival and we walked out to greet our tired troopers. Both kids said, "Man, it's hot." After welcoming them and congratulating Kevin, Ray gave them grief for being California woosies. "If you can't take the heat…"

"Yeah, yeah. We're not used to running an air conditioner. And here's Rusty." Kevin released an armful of wiggling muscular puppy. White gray body with the bulls-eye markings, Rusty sniffed, barked, jumped, scampered, and peed. Fearless, he ran circles in the field next to our house and pooped with abandon. He was bigger than I expected with way more energy. Plus he had that pit bull face; those teeth, that jowl, and the power to tear someone from limb to limb. I was re-thinking my generosity. I watched him gnaw on

93

our tiny crepe myrtle tree. At least it wasn't one of our leg bones.

"Well, you're back in Texas, Kevin. Far from an ocean breeze." I added my two cents. "Are you hungry? Your dad has enchiladas in the oven. Chris should be here soon."

"That sounds wonderful." Kevin swayed a bit. He was excited to be home, but weary. "Now Joanne, is it okay for us to stay? We have a cage for Rusty and he sleeps through the night."

This was my chance to renege. I paused, the sound of Rusty's teeth chomping on his stick echoed in my head. His puppy eyes had a gleam of potential evil, not that they glowed red but they could. To break the awkward silence, I lied. "Yes. I told your father to tell you it would be fine. It's just one night. If it were a week, I might have issues."

"He'll be good." Rusty leaped around Kevin asking to play, and Kevin addressed him. "Won't you be a good boy? Yeah, that's my boy." Rusty clamped down on a stick and held on while Kevin swung him around.

He's a puppy, a mere puppy. I, nervous and on edge, went inside to set the table for dinner

"Kevin, I do have to ask that the dog stay out back while we eat. I can't have him underfoot during dinner."

As I scowled, he grinned. "Oh, but I was going to feed him at the table. He'd sit on my lap," and herded Rusty out the back door. "Sorry fella, behave."

At the dinner table, we dug in to our Tex-Mex feast and caught up on all of the news. We talked over each other, asked questions, joked, and enjoyed dinner together. Chris got up to mix margaritas. Maria rose for a refill and then paused.

"I think I saw something out front." She had a puzzled look on her face.

"Oh we've had some big squirrels scampering about." I dismissed her concern.

"No, that's Rusty." She pushed her chair back and ran for the front door. Kevin dropped his fork and followed. Ray stood and drew the lacy drapes back for a better view. Sure enough. Proud as punch, Rusty trotted by the window. With that perky face, he almost grinned, and then ran to escape the clutches of his masters. It was a game. He jogged, dodged, and evaded. Finally, Kevin leaped and engulfed him in a hug. Rusty licked Kevin's face; unaware of the trouble he was in.

"So, how did he get out front?" I asked. Ray turned from the window, frowned, and marched out the back door. Kevin and Maria with an armful of Rusty re-entered the house. Maria scolded Rusty, "Bad boy. You aren't supposed to roam around." They hauled him to the back, and I followed.

"Kevin, Rusty chewed through the wood fence back here. Look at this." Exasperated, Ray stood with his hands on his hips. He swept one hand toward the gaping hole. "He worked fast. The fence is weak in spots and he found one. I have slats in the shed. Go get my hammer in the toolbox." Ray stomped to the shed. I stayed back, away from my fuming husband, away from the destructive dog. In the meantime, Rusty played. He

95

gamboled about the back yard and nudged another fence area. He growled, ready to chew some more. Maria corralled him and held on. It was all she could do to contain his puppy energy.

The sound of hammering echoed and soon, the fence was repaired. Ray attached a few extra pieces at other weak areas. "Sorry, dad." Kevin kept apologizing.

"Hey, obviously the fence had some issues. Let's get back in and finish dinner." Ray shrugged, practically philosophical.

"Oh, wow, look at this chair." I pointed to one of our green striped patio chairs that was unstuffed. Now, I wasn't feeling quite so charitable. White cushion litter blew like cotton balls under the patio table.

Kevin hung his head. "Sorry, again and again." Maria gave Rusty a swat and shoved his nose at the chair. "No, Rusty. Bad boy. Don't chew the chair cushions."

I was annoyed, but what could I do? He was a puppy in a strange area, and he had lots of teeth to sharpen. At least he hadn't approached me to start gnawing. I wasn't putting an arm or hand near the jaws of death. That was his exercise, to bite and chew up our home. We had no idea how quickly he could work his destruction. Kevin decided to get the cage and set it up. Rusty cowered and whimpered. He tried to dig in his heels and resist, but Kevin won. He found Rusty's toy bone which silenced his whining.

"One puppy wreaked havoc in less than an hour. What will happen when you have kids?" I asked.

"I doubt they'll chew through the fence." Poor Kevin. He apologized again and poured a mug of margarita. "So, after dinner, I'm taking Maria to visit my mom and sister. Then I've got some friends to see. We'll take Rusty with us. Unless, Joanne, do you want to babysit?" Yeah, very funny. Kevin continued, "Dad, keep the front door unlocked. It'll be late."

We cleaned up dinner dishes while the kids prepared to leave. They came into the kitchen with Rusty on his leash. Rusty panted, tried to leap, but Kevin jerked him back. "We're heading out. Thanks for dinner. I'm so glad to be back in Tex……..no, Rusty, no." Rusty piddled on the kitchen floor. Ray grabbed some paper towels for Kevin. Once again, Kevin apologized. "He never does this indoors, I swear."

"What time do you move to the apartment?" I sorta joked and looked at the kitchen clock.

"Maybe we should leave now and park the u-haul outside their gates." Kevin said.

I patted him on the back. "You just gave me more evidence in case your Dad ever decides he wants a dog. Have fun. Gonna be hot tomorrow. Moving at end of May isn't the best timing. See ya."

They left and we shut the front door. I leaned against it, worn out from the bedlam.

"Holy crap, Ray. Are we gonna survive a pit bull staying in our guest room?"

Chapter 15: Make Yourself at Home

One early March Saturday morning, I opened the family room drapes as usual and gazed out at our backyard that includes a swimming pool. It was shaping up to be a pretty day, blue sky and brisk but not cold. With no wind, the pool was glass until two sets of whirring wings glided in for a landing. One brilliant green head glimmered in the sunlight. A mallard duck and his mate decided to forego the pleasure of Bedford's public Chisholm Park up the street. Guess it was too noisy and crowded. Instead, the duo paddled our pool and then settled onto its deck, sunning and napping.

I snapped pictures through the window, and even opened the backdoor quietly to get a good zoom-in photo. The ducks never flinched.

They made a lovely pair and appeared well behaved. Well, other than pooping on our tile, peeing in our pool, and leaving feathers for the skimmer. I suppose I was expected to overlook those indiscretions, while admiring the beauty of their effortless glide, the noble turn of his head, and her discreet position behind him.

"Do you think they're going to stay? It makes me nervous," I said to Ray as we both peered out the window.

"What is your problem?" he asked. "They landed, they're swimming, they'll move on. Especially if our friend the hawk starts flying his circle pattern overhead."

"True. But, do you think they're nesting? You need to get out there and check the shrubs."

"Yes, dear." Ray's peevish tone indicated his displeasure at me. Nonetheless he walked out later, after the ducks had flown off, to scope out the bushes and look for suspicious nesting materials. When he came in, he said, "I bet they won't return. Just passing through."

"We'll see."

Sunday morning, same time, the ducks made a graceful landing and quacked contentedly as they cruised the pool perimeter.

"See, they plan on living here. Why here?" I stood with my arms out, waving them around.

Ray didn't even look up from his paper. "Look how nice our backyard is. Quiet, peaceful. The water has no chemicals right now for winter. Except for lack of fish to eat, our pool is an oasis."

I snorted and decided to walk outside. The ducks were on deck at the time, stretching their legs and ruffling feathers. I stepped closer and they both quacked and plunged into the pool. As if by ignoring me I would go away, they never looked back but paddled quickly to the opposite end of the pool. I stood and watched. They fretted a bit, but then relaxed when they saw I wasn't planning on a polar bear swim. I clapped my hands. They stared at me. I clapped again and walked closer, heading towards the diving board. With that, they flapped mightily and flew off in a whoosh of water drips, quacks, and a spare feather swirling down.

Morning and soon early evenings, the ducks made their appearance and ruled the backyard. I was certain she was laying eggs somewhere, but she never acted flummoxed or pulled the old broken wing trick when I strolled outside. Instead, the ducks continued to poop, quack, swim, and leave on a regular schedule.

I had reached equilibrium with the ducks. They could enjoy the tranquility for another month. Then the chlorine level would be rising in preparation for summer pool season. I assumed that would drive them away and said as much to Ray as we once again stood looking out our back window.

"This place is like an aviary, Ray," I said.

"What now?"

"Those darn fat doves are determined to nest up on the little porch speakers. They've even knocked down the foil on the left one," I said as I pointed at my crumpled warning.

'They'll give up."

"Doubt it. And they are scary. Swooping and chirping at me. They act really annoyed when I step outside. Scared the crap out of me the other day."

"Doves coo, not chirp. And I'm sure you scared them. I'll put the foil back up. It will deter the nest building."

"Well, I have to keep sweeping up their twigs and junk. They aren't neat homebuilders, that's for sure. Ducks, doves, what's next? An ostrich?"

Ray smiled and chucked me under the chin. "You're a birdbrain, you know that."

Chapter 16: Aquatic Life – Snort & Snorkel Fin Flap

Not on my life to-do list: Swim With Dolphins. Could have done it in Mexico, opted out. Loved watching dolphins cavort alongside the tour boat in Milford Sound, New Zealand. Graceful and fabulous, but the urge to grab a fin and frolic isn't there.

Ray scuba dives and I love to hear his adventures and see his pictures. However, the thought of a shark circling overhead in Belize or the view of a moray eel flashing his triple sharp teeth required me to increase insurance on my spouse.

In theory, I should want to scuba dive, too. As a little girl, I swam with vigor through the years to earn patches – Tadpole, Minnow, Fish, Flying Fish, and Shark. I achieved it all in the over-chlorinated waters of the Lansdale YMCA. Four tiled self-contained pool walls. Therein lies my problem. Scuba involves open water, current, and wild creatures (not that unruly eight year olds didn't count as such at the Y). Plus, and this is the deal breaker, I hate hearing myself breathe.

Ray brought home tanks one day to give me a mini-lesson. I loathed it, hyperventilated, and spat out the mouthpiece, gulping in overheated Texas air. "Try it again and just breathe in and out. You're gonna get air. Stay calm," said Ray pretending to be a nurturing teacher. I tried again and claustrophobia overcame me. I was not getting enough air. I just knew it. Un-oxygenated brain cells dripped out of my ears, floating away to turn into brain coral. (You didn't know that could happen, did you?)

Besides breathing, vision is crucial and mine is quite suspect. Remove my glasses and I become the village idiot in a corner. I can't see anything clearly beyond my nose. Astigmatism and near-sightedness combine to challenge my viewing pleasure. Without glasses, the world is a gauzy blur, hazily lacking imperfection. I once asked my ophthalmologist my number and she replied, "You have finger vision. You can see movement." Hence, I tend to scope out our backyard pool prior to a plunge. Glasses on, I walk the perimeter looking for frogs, spiders, snakes, and any other creature that should not be swimming with me. I've learned from experience, and do not seek surprise face-to- face encounters with the above.

It is difficult to skim out the nasty in lakes or oceans. Thus, if I'm on a boat on a lake, I tend to stay on the boat. I'm just not good at murky, or surprises tickling my skin. However, I did participate in two snorkel adventures.

In Hawaii, we went out on a big tour boat that stopped in a sanctioned marine park. I took the plunge along with everyone else. I'll be honest. Still had problems with the breathing out thing. I tended to skim along the top of the ocean water, lift my head to breath, and lower. The fish in Hawaii were so colorful that even I could see them. Yellows, reds, stripes. The brilliance was breathtaking, and it was pretty cool.

The boat took us out to the ancient turtle area. Again, so big, even I could see them underwater. Their barnacled shells and wrinkled skin attested to their age. Slow on land, they paddled with grace and ease under water, huge tanks floating in paradise. I didn't touch any, didn't feel the need to, and was perfectly content to let the underwater scenery stay serene.

A snorkel trip in Mexico was disappointing. We were hauled out to a reef in a rickety vessel. It looked like a pirate shipwreck already. Dumped overboard with minimal instruction, the goal was to snorkel and move along with the group. Well, there was a berserk jet stream. No time to view the reef or aquatic life. It was swim for your life and don't drown. We were tired troupers by the time we dragged ourselves back onto the boat. One person reported seeing something cool. The rest of us were tired and annoyed.

That's the extent of my life aquatic. I'll let others line up to befriend Flipper. I'll wave goodbye to Ray as he packs his scuba gear, and I'll up the ante on that life insurance. Wriggle my toes in the sand or visit an aquarium.

Chapter 17: Turtle Laps

Remember Chris and Kevin found the box turtle at the creek, brought him home, and vowed he wanted to live with us. Ray kept sending them back to the creek, until one day I found the turtle half-alive rolled in a Halloween costume. Fortunately that trick-or-treater survived. Our visitor must have spread the word, and a turtle cousin showed up for a swim.

It's dangerous to come home from work first. That means I have to bring in the recycle bin, clear soaking pots from the kitchen sink, notice and do odd jobs, and deal with creatures. That includes the bugs in death throes on the floor, doves swishing wings in haste as they flee their new nest by the back door, and me squinting to see what could be in the pool. As I step outside, I pray that I'm seeing a shadow. The sun glinting off the water must be creating an optical illusion. I step closer and have found a snake wiggling in the deep end, a mouse perched precariously on the pool hose, and a rabbit paddling, desperate to hop out of hot water (it is Texas, the pool's like a spa in the summer).

This particular day, much to my dismay, was a turtle. Rather than a domesticated box turtle gone astray, this fellow was slim, dark brown, and fast. Guess he was tired of the creek life, took a hike, and fell into our pool. Or maybe, he'd always wanted to do a double header off a diving board. His city cousin had bragged, so the country cousin investigated. Either way, he was swimming laps like an Olympian. Nothing I could do except choose to not swim that afternoon, and await Ray.

"What are you doing inside?" he asked as he arrived home from work and sorted through mail.

"We have a visitor," I said. "You know how I don't want to swim with dolphins. Well, I've decided against turtles too. There's one in the pool."

"Oh yeah?" Ray's shoulders slumped and he strolled out back to assess the situation. "He's pretty fast." Ray got the net pole and made a few half-hearted attempts to snag the turtle. It was quite evident that wasn't going to happen. Ray gave up, went inside to change clothes, and read the comics. Part of the evening was spent chasing the turtle. He'd slow down, as if to allow Ray to catch up, and then zoom away to the other end of the pool. Ray finally found some material in the shed to build a small ramp in the shallow end.

"He'll get tired sooner or later and crawl out. It's up to him to find this path."

With that, Ray doused the lights and we went to bed. The turtle did not invite friends over for a night swim, no raucous music and no chatter. Not a splash.

106

The next morning, prior to breakfast, we stepped outside to check on our guest. The pool was empty. He must have hauled himself up the ramp to head home. I had Ray check the bushes, just in case, but there was no sign of our buddy. Not even a turtle dropping. Ray was proud of his engineering masterpiece, and I was relieved that the turtle was not floating upside down in the pool, overcome by chemical poisoning. All parties were happy.

Until ... I came home from work that afternoon. The beach umbrella waved in a hot summer breeze; there might as well have been party music blasting and beer on ice. He wasn't riding the pool float. Instead, our turtle invader swam in lazy circles. I walked closer to the edge. He saw my shadow, sped up, and swam away. Ray was going to be thrilled. I thought about calling him, but why ruin his drive home? Let him still bask in his alleged victory. He'd find out soon enough.

I sat on the patio and read, more to give a false sense of calm. Ray changed into his swimsuit. Paper, soda, and snacks in hand, he said, "Hey, how was your day?"

"Fine enough until I got home."

"Oh?" He paused. "Oh." The tone lowered and he turned and walked to the edge. "Well, dang it. Why'd he go back in?"

"Guess it's refreshing. I don't know what you're planning to do, but ..."

Ray stopped me, " I know, I know. I have to get him out of there."

"What are you going to do?"

"Don't know yet, but he'll be gone soon."

Ray pretended to work on the crossword puzzle, but the whole time he contemplated our problem. He finally leaped up, unlocked the gate, got a bowl and set it on the diving board. He then went after that turtle with the net pole. It was a tussle, but Ray nabbed him. He had the turtle pinned to the wall and slowly inched him up the side. "I need something thin, like a tray or cookie sheet," Ray called to me. "Hurry."

I ran inside, clattered around the cupboards, and came out with our scroungiest sheet.

"Over here. Bring the bowl, too. I'm almost to the top and you need to position the sheet between the wall and the turtle." Ray was red in the face and tiring from the exertion. "Okay, now." There was enough space, and I managed to slide the sheet without dropping it or falling in the pool. Ray somehow flipped the turtle on his back into the bowl and clapped the sheet on top. "Back to the creek, buddy boy," Ray murmured to his nemesis. "I need my flip-flops." I scurried to get them and lined them up for Ray to step in and go. I gave him a kiss and he said, "I'll be back." He headed out the gate and marched toward the creek, a few hundred yards away.

"Alone," I called out to him. He gave me his rolled eyes, yeah thanks look, and I waved.

Ray returned, locked the gate, and put fresh chemicals in the pool. The next morning dawned clear and no turtle in sight. I'm guessing he won't be coming back due to our lack of hospitality. Plus

the summer pool temperature rose daily. He
avoided becoming turtle soup.

Chapter 18: The Swedish Swan Incident

"Shriek, inte. Shriek, inte." In her panic, Lisa resorted to Swedish. I tried to stop shouting, but my fear flew out of my mouth in a high-pitched scream. The flap of large white wings threatened boat upheaval. We clung to our paddles.

"Why the heck did I come to Sweden, anyhow?" I thought. "I might die here today."

When I filled out the exchange student profile, I checked the box for 'no pets'. Smoking – hell yeah, I'll inhale second hand unfiltered cigarette. Outdoor plumbing – sure. Situated next to a nuclear power plant – no problem. Animals – oh, I've got a problem all right. Sophomore year, 1974, was almost over and I awaited news of placement for summer exchange student. My first choice was France, since I studied French II. Second choice was anywhere. I wanted a summer abroad, to travel, live with a family, and not be stuck in North Wales, PA. Not quite sixteen, I couldn't drive or

110

get a job. Summer at home would be a drag. It was time to get away.

Finally got a call from the Youth For Understanding coordinator, "How about a summer in Sweden?"

"Huh?" That wasn't France, but I wasn't picky anymore.

"French selection is difficult. There aren't many families open for summer only. However, we have this family in Sweden whose daughter is headed to the U.S. in the fall. They've agreed to take an American student, so Elisabet can work on her English and prepare for her year in California. Here's your chance. Congratulations."

I said yes and a whirlwind of preparations began. First, check the map and reacquaint myself with Stockholm, Sweden. Ah, tucked up north with Norway, Finland, and Denmark. Buy a phrasebook and practice words that have lots of js, ws, and weird symbols hovering over the vowels. Complete finals, pack, and enjoy a bon voyage party thrown by a good friend. Travel day, mid-June, arrived amidst a mixture of nerves and excitement. I'd flown before but not overseas. I'd stayed overnight at friends' homes, but never lived for two months with another family. Not only that, but foreigners, not relatives. This was going to be amazing and scary.

Lori, age five, cried, "Don't go away," and for a second I had a pang of dread. What if this new family hated me? Did they speak English? What if I got on the wrong plane? Was their food gross? What have I gotten myself into? Kinda too late now. We were at the airport gate: Mom, Dad, David, and Lori, and the mumbled announcement gave my flight number for boarding. Passport and carry-on, I hugged everyone, gulped back tears, and set off for a summer in Sweden.

Philadelphia to New York to Copenhagen, and finally Stockholm. There had been delays along the way. Exhausted, I stumbled from the plane and looked for someone who might be looking for me. At this point, I definitely resembled my hideous passport picture. A very tall man with a long face and reddish hair approached me, along with a short slender woman. She had sharp features and a nervous habit of tucking her brown hair behind her right ear. He smiled and glanced at a photo in his hand. "Joanne Crowther?" I nodded and they both shook my hand introducing themselves rather formally, "Arne and Karin Wickman."

"You are well and had safe travels?" she asked. I replied that everything was fine except for being so tired. It was near midnight and I was jetlagged. Didn't sleep the night before, and couldn't rest on the plane due to anticipation. Now that I was here, I was ready to collapse. They do speak proper English. They chatted to me and to each other as we waited at baggage claim. Once my huge bag was in hand, we found their Saab, and headed to their home in Bromma, a suburb of Stockholm. Everything was dark, other than the highway, so there was no point looking out the window. I concentrated on staying awake. We pulled into a driveway, and like a zombie I staggered into the house. I declined food or drink. "Thank you, but I'm ready for bed."

Karin showed me my room and the bathroom. "Sleep well, we're very glad you shall spend the summer with us." I murmured good night, dug out my nightgown, and fell into bed. Didn't even brush my teeth.

Awoke to a quiet house and unsure of the time, I peered out my window. A sunny garden view appeared promising. I rummaged through my suitcase, vowing to get situated later, and pulled out jeans, a t-shirt, and underwear. Opened my door and a panther glanced at me with one lazy green eye. This huge black cat blocked my exit. I stepped over it gingerly and headed to the bathroom. It never moved a paw.

Showered and refreshed I listened for voices or sounds of life. Peered into rooms, walked downstairs, and arrived at the kitchen. A young woman hummed and put dishes away. I said hello and she turned with a warm smile. Shoulder length brown hair and clear blue eyes in a friendly face. "Marta, ja," and she extended her hand. I shook it and said, "Joanne." Her English was hesitant but I figured out that she was the housekeeper. Arne and Karin were at work, Anders at soccer, Gustav at summer math camp, and Elisabet would be back shortly. Breakfast was a soft-boiled egg or cereal. Rice Krispies snap, crackle, and pop in Swedish, too. As I ate a final scoop, the back door opened and in came a Swedish model. Elisabet, at sixteen, was tall with long straight blonde hair, blue eyes, tan legs, a lovely face, and a perfect figure. A

113

Swedish dream, she'd fit in great on the beaches of California.

"Oh, Joanne, I'm so glad you are here. I must learn everything American." From Elisabet to Lisa, in an instant we were best friends and summer sisters. Her rapid fire English was Oxford proper, and she insisted on some slang words immediately. I gave my Philly, "Yo, whatcha' doin'" and we were off and running. After another tour of the house and yard, plus a proper introduction to Sven the cat (who now to my consternation sprawled on my bed), we grabbed bikes and rode to the train station for a jaunt into Stockholm.

My head swiveled and I admired the pristine towns and cities. The twenty-minute train ride ended at the main terminal and I stepped out to start one of the best days of my life. An entrancing city, Stockholm offered old section Gamla Stan, with its tiny streets and stone buildings in contrast with gleaming modern towers overlooking the harbor. Water everywhere. Boats cruised the harbor and inlets. We strolled the streets, peered into shop windows filled with Orrefors glass, bought ice cream cones, and watched old men play chess in the local park. Flowers overflowed window planters. Statues, sculptures, and fountains decorated every nook of the city. Plus, gorgeous healthy Swedes made the city look like a magazine cover. The Swedish babble encircled me. Little white haired toddlers called, "Mama," in Swedish. Everyone appeared happy and content, since most folks were on holiday. June begins the summer slowdown, and a majority of Swedes hop aboard

114

their boats, or head to their vacation homes. So close to the Arctic Circle, the winters are long. Thus, Swedes worship their days in the sun and I learned that upcoming June 21st was a huge festival day to celebrate the longest day of sunshine in the year.

Minimal animal encounters in the city. There were dogs on leashes in the parks, and everyone behaved. At one restaurant, Lisa and I stopped for lunch, and I was startled to realize a woman had a little dog in a purse at her table. Common in Europe, small dogs are an accessory - quiet and unobtrusive they travel with their owner, not a growl to be heard.

Late afternoon I confessed I was tired. My travel day hit me and this one day of walking about Stockholm was the final blow. Fatigued, I fell asleep on the train. Lisa had to shake me awake at our stop. Once home, I got in a nap after removing Sven from my bed. He was going to be a problem. This cat hovered at my door and would appear underfoot wherever I'd walk in the house. He didn't seem to go to any family members. I never saw him on a lap, but he was gunning for me.

Revived, I kept my eyes open for dinner and met the rest of the family. More blondies, Anders, at twelve, was the athlete and demonstrated his soccer skills in the backyard. He was shy about his English and we didn't talk much all summer. Gustav, age seven, was a math genius. He loved to count and propose problems. He and I spent the summer on numbers, counting in Swedish and English. Gustav mastered his part better than me.

My first Swedish dinner involved fish and lots of questions. Finally, Arne tapped his spoon on his beer mug, "We have all summer. Look at poor Joanne, almost asleep in her soup. Dessert now, but no more questions to her. We'll enjoy family time tomorrow on the boat." With that, Lisa and Anders switched to Swedish. My guess was an argument on driving the boat. They were competitive and sibling rivalry sounds the same worldwide. I enjoyed my slice of torte and excused myself to go to bed.

No sign of Sven on the bed, under the bed, or under my covers. I checked the closets to be sure. That cat was tall enough to reach a door handle. I shut my door, did lights out, and collapsed into an exhausted but content sleep, only to be roused by Anders pounding on my door and saying something in Swedish. "Boat" came through and another day of adventure dawned.

My summer in Sweden flew by and I experienced a lot. Plenty of museum visits, castles to explore, and, from a distance, I had a chance to see the King of Sweden on his royal yacht as Arne steered us through the archipelago. Arne, Karin, Gustav, and I had a long weekend trip to Norway. We saw a herd of reindeer running out along a glacier. Crisp, clean air and wondrous snowy mountains. I loved Norway and had the best ice cream at a kiosk on top of one peak. Shivering and eating a vanilla creamy concoction, I was on top of the world. The family was so kind and wanted me to explore as much of Scandinavia as possible.

Only a short time left for me, and also, Lisa would be heading to California. As a last hurrah, the family packed up for a week at their vacation home a few hours outside of Stockholm. It belonged to the grandmother, but any family member could use it. Rustic and charming, filled with Swedish antiques, the house didn't have running water and there was an outhouse. Not a big fan of roughing it, I enjoyed the countryside but missed amenities. Perhaps this part of the trip was designed to get me excited to return home to America.

Anyway, we bathed in the cold lake water and took turns pumping the well for our cooking water. Lisa and I went to parties and drank beer. I was a novelty and kids practiced speaking English with me, mimicking my accent. No responsibilities and no curfews. We walked everywhere – just had to watch for Swedish cow patties in the fields.

The week was almost over. Saturday, we munched on a breakfast cake and debated our entertainment for the day. "We could go into town," I said without conviction. It was a small town and we'd pretty much covered it from one end to the other. "Or how about biking."

"No, Anders and Gustav took off this morning on them. They were going fishing," Lisa said.

She turned towards the living room and spoke in Swedish. "Papa, may Joanne and I go out in the boat? I haven't taken her by the little waterfall yet."

Arne replied with something and she answered. Satisfied, he returned to his paper. Lisa started opening cupboards and talking. "We must pack a picnic. Find us some Cokes and get our beach bag from the hallway." She muttered a bit.

"No herring." That was my only request. I never did acquire a taste for Sweden's national food. They put those things on pizza, for God's sake. Ugh. We gathered up towels, sunscreen, and our lunch. I followed Lisa on the twisty path to the rowboat, and tossed our pile into the boat. Strapped into life vests, and eager to see the waterfall, we unhitched the boat, pushed, and set sail under our own power. It didn't take too long to coordinate our oar strokes and we made headway. Sort of a combination lake/river, there was some current to fight. However, with minimal wind and no one else in sight, we'd stop for breaks and drift. Blue sky, 80s, the slap of a fish or the croak of a frog. "You're going to miss this, Lisa. California has the ocean and lakes, but there's always other people around and a lot more activity. I didn't think there really was places like this – so calm and peaceful," I slowed my rowing and gazed at the view.

"Ja, I know. I've begun to feel a bit anxious about going for a whole school year. You were smart. Travel and visit, but no studies," Lisa grimaced.

"You'll be the smartest one in your class, trust me. And your English is way better than lots of American kids." I reassured her. "Guys will be following you like it's a parade. Now, that could

118

hurt your grades...partying and dating in California. Sweden has a rep for nudity and wildness."

"Get out of here," Lisa used her newfound slang.

"For real. You'll be popular but be careful."

"Exchange students have rules. They'll keep track of me, I'm sure. I wish I could come to your house. My American family's father is an Army Colonel. Do you think I'll have to salute constantly?" She snapped off a crisp one, and we got the giggles.

Rowing and laughing, we raised a ruckus. Anyone or anything could hear us. The lake had narrowed into more of a river and we concentrated on paddling. Ahead was another wide open area and I pointed, "Look, is that a swan?"

"Ach, I forgot about them." Lisa untied and tied back her ponytail. I'd learned to recognize that worry tic. We rowed quietly and approached the opening. Whoosh. Huge white wings flapped over us. It didn't dive bomb, but it was close. We glided into a swan party as uninvited guests. My delight at seeing these graceful birds disappeared after the first hiss and angry snap of a neck. Increasingly disturbed at our presence, a wave of white wings slapped at the boat. They came at us from all sides, paddling by or flying low. Honking, hissing, squawking. The swans would reconvene, talk amongst themselves, and then spread out to hinder our movement.

"These birds are gonna peck us. Oh shit." I flailed and nearly dropped my oar. Tipped

119

precariously, I held on and we steadied the boat. I smelled a fishy swampy odor and decided it wasn't me; it must have been all of the swans. Another swan made a fly/jump overhead. Again, I ducked and this time, Lisa lost her balance. She thunked down hard, scattering towels and our lunch, and glared at me over her shoulder.

"Hold on and paddle hard. We have to get out to the middle. There's baby swans and the mothers aren't happy with us." Lisa sounded calm. However, reseated, she had her head down and concentrated on her stroke.

A swan wound up and ran/walked on the water towards the boat. Wings beat rapidly and it hissed. The bird was fast and I stopped to cower deeper into the boat. I could hear screaming. It was me and I tried to think. Stop screaming. I can't. You have to. But I'm incapable of quiet. OH MY GOD, that swan is attacking the boat. My piercing screams and paralyzing collapse into the seats caused more chaos. Lisa yelled in Swedish at me, at the birds, and back at me again. The boat rocked and we took on some water. I couldn't move. I should move, but where. How are we supposed to row out of this mess? I hate Sweden. This lake sucks. I despise swans. I wonder what Mom and Dad are doing. They'd be so sad if I was pecked to death by birds. Hot and cold at the same time, I realized I sat in a puddle in the boat. I crawled back to my station and lifted my head. I gasped for air, moaned, and hiccupped. Then I couldn't stop my hiccups, so I tried to hold my breath. But I couldn't do that since I was breathing so hard from my panic.

Lisa sat in the middle of the boat and moved her oar from side to side in an attempt to keep forward motion. Our interminable crawl to open water was slowed by the rocking of the boat. In my haste to hide, I'd kicked open our picnic lunch that had been thrown to the boat floor. A Coke bottle clunked to the deck and rolled underfoot. Lisa hit me with her oar and shouted, "Get up and row. I can't do this alone."

Snapped out of my nightmare, I did stop screeching and re-took my oar. My foot squished a sandwich. I blinked back tears and saw that Lisa's face was streaked too. One or two swans fluttered nearby, reminding us we were in their territory. We were finally far enough along into open water to be less of a threat. Most swans resumed their regular activity. The two bullies arched their necks as if daring us to return.

"Um, how do we get home? Are we gonna have to row back through that mess?" Chastened, I spoke in a hushed tone. I didn't want to stir up more birds.

Lisa was mad at me. Her face was flushed and hair spilled out of her ponytail. Her blue eyes were cold and calculating. "God, you didn't do a thing back there. What's wrong with you?"

"I couldn't help it. I didn't mean to do nothing. I couldn't move. Those freakin'swans were scary. We coulda been killed."

"No, we weren't going to die. This water isn't that deep. It's good you didn't tip over the boat in your spaz out. I might have killed you then, not the birds."

"I'm sorry. I really am."

"Well, we're almost to the waterfall and then there's a dock place. We're on the opposite side of the lake. I'll call Papa to pick us up. He'll do it since you're here."

We rowed the rest of the way in silence, ate our lunch in silence with a view of the waterfall, and quietly docked the rowboat. Lisa called her Papa and he rescued us. He attempted some conversation in the car, but gave that up quickly. He didn't want to be hissed at.

Beautiful, graceful, and mean. Swans are swans, whether in America or Sweden. I contend I could have died that day in an international boat incident.

Chapter 19: Don't Stare Down the Wombat

February 2005

G'day, mate, indeed! Ray and I enjoyed summer down under with a trip to Australia and New Zealand. Shivering in Texas, we boarded a plane, flew for a zillion hours, and arrived in Sydney to bask in sunshine and warm temperatures. It's so cliché to call a trip the dream of a lifetime, but our time in the Pacific was magical. No tsunamis, no labor strikes, no flight delays, no lost luggage, and no illness for three weeks. We traveled over five thousand miles in and around and between the two countries.

Danger lurked. Australia is home to some of the deadliest spiders in the world. Poisonous jellyfish dangle evil tentacles at the Great Barrier Reef where Ray dove for a day. Kangaroos have enough leg strength to kill a man with one kick. Dingoes are wild pack animals (think Elaine on *Seinfeld*, "The dingo ate your baby.") And finally, there's the wombat, an ugly bear-like creature with large teeth. Australia is a wild, amazing country with unique animals roaming its countryside, and Ray and I were there to soak it all in.

Our first adventure was at the Sydney Aquarium. We saw huge fierce sharks that ply the coastal waters. Their tank had a walk through so we felt as if we were in a diving bell. Sharks roamed overhead and underfoot which was eerie. Gleaming rows of teeth glistened, fortunately behind thick glass.

In another room, the colorful jellyfish with stingers of death floated aimlessly in separated tanks. They looked so harmless. We also walked above a crocodile habitat. The crocs sat, partially submerged in a pool, bored with the day. The sign read, "If the fall doesn't kill you, the crocodile will." Indeed, one snap of that mighty jaw...I shuddered at the thought. I'd seen enough nature programs. Crocodiles are fast and relentless. They will not release captured prey.

After peering at sea creatures that could kill, Ray was still game to scuba dive at the Great Barrier Reef, so we flew to Cairns and then bussed up to Port Douglas. Fortunately, because deaths would deter tourists, Australia installed huge amounts of netting around their dive platforms to keep out sharks and jellyfish. I was content to stay and play at the platform. Took a Captain Nemo submersible ride. The delicacy of the reef combined with the rainbow of colors enthralled.

Meanwhile, Ray swam for his life. Oh, no sharks chased him; the killer current that day that wore him out. From the sound of things, I saw far more fish than Ray and my helicopter ride gave me a better overview of the reef area, the intense layers of azure blue waters. We survived the Great Barrier Reef with nary a bite or sting.

Onward to Ayers Rock and the forbidding Australian Outback. Death strikes here in the form of heat and merciless flies. I exaggerate. The flies don't actually kill you, but their incessant pestering could drive you insane. I'm sure there were creatures hiding in corners of the Rock, but again, we stayed on the path and nothing pounced. Sunrise and sunset at Ayers Rock were stupendous.

Our travel pace increased and we were back on board a flight to Melbourne. I had time to read more travel literature and the wombat overshadowed the koala in my mind. I wanted to see one, yet fear niggled my brain. I stashed my brochures for later as we landed. Our day trip to Port Phillips Island gave us a chance to see a penguin parade. I'm fine with animals in a controlled environment and Australia tourism prepared everything to protect the penguins from mankind and vice versa. As sunset, we plopped on bleachers. No cameras allowed and security means it. They nab phone cameras or anything with a light source. Dusk and the murmur of conversation hushed as we scanned the beach for sign of movement. Sure enough, one lone penguin plopped out of the water and hesitantly waddled to shore. After a day of swimming and feeding, the little penguins were so full of fish, they'd tip over at times. Following the same path they've followed for thousands of years, the penguins found their burrows to rest and hide from bigger birds or predators.

One, then a group of five, and then up to twenty penguins at a time chattered and waddled to their nests. It was compelling and fascinating. If a bird flew overhead, they scurried faster to escape danger. We strolled on a boardwalk and peered over to see the penguins enter and exit the burrows. Baby penguins were pushed along to their respective parents, and like a child lost in the mall, one poor youngster chirped sad, confused and tired.

No marauding penguins. They were too fat to move too quickly or attack anything. Our night at the Penguin Parade proved entertaining and safe. The only thing that hurt was our butts from sitting on those darn bleachers for two hours.

So far, Australia was tame. Any danger was behind glass or nets. Then there was a wildlife park. We were greeted at the gate by a ranger and a dingo. "Welcome. We hope you enjoy your day here. Oops, no, young lady. Don't try to pet the dingo." A young girl, encouraged by her parents, had reached out to stroke it. "This isn't a dog. It's a fierce scavenger. Clare, here, is old and cranky." Indeed, the dingo bared its teeth. As the ranger opened the gate and took tickets, I gave Clare a wide berth. Maybe she shouldn't have been part of the welcoming committee.

Walking through a natural habitat area, the goal was to spot as many koala bears as possible. These languid creatures are so loopy from chewing on eucalyptus leaves all day that they don't move.

126

Honestly. They sleep twenty or more hours in a row. If they do wake, they are drugged and blink in slow motion.

The park rangers had a koala available to pet and the whole bus group lined up. "You have to pet the koala," said Ray, his hands on his hips, sunglasses pushed up on top of his head, camera about his neck. The only things missing were black socks and sandals. We were such tourists.

"I guess it'll be okay," I hesitated. Why do these thoughts flash through my brain? What if this koala was finally fed up with being petted and decided to rampage? Koalas have sharp claws? What if I met the koala that had been through rehab and was cranky from eucalyptus withdrawal? It could happen. I'd be part of an international wildlife park incident.

Ray and I lined up behind everyone else. The bear looked bored and sleepy, half-propped in the ranger's arms. We got closer and I felt a bit anxious, but the koala hadn't moved. It wasn't waving its little arms, kicking its feet, or growling. Ray had his turn, petted the bear, and posed for a picture. My turn. It's okay. Nothing will happen. You're in Australia and this is way cool. Tentative, I put out my hand and touched the top back of the koala's head and quickly withdrew. The fur was fluffy and he didn't move. It really did look like a stuffed animal. "You didn't give me a chance to take a picture. Pet the damn thing and stand there. Smile," Ray instructed me. I'd concentrated on watching the bear for sudden movement. I didn't have time to pose.

"There." I petted the koala for more than a second, glanced at Ray and flashed a smile. Click, he got it. There's proof that I petted, not hugged, a wild animal in Australia.

Out of Koala Kountry, we walked to the kangaroo station. There we entered a gate and walked amongst these tall, odd creatures. This freaked me out. "We're too close. What if they kick?"

Ray stopped and looked at me, then waved his arms in a wide circle. "Do these kangaroos look like they give a shit that we're walking here? Hell, no. They're well fed and kinda fat. They know a good gig and they aren't going to attack. Sheesh." He continued to stroll and stopped to snap a picture of a mama and her roo. Ungainly legs stuck out of her pouch. She was busy getting her brood situated. I stayed in the middle of the path, close enough to observe, yet out of the path of a wayward hop Ray ventured off to look and take pictures. "C'mere," he called to me. "C'mon, you need to see this." Gingerly I stepped off the path to a corner of the area. There were some kangaroo toddlers hopping playfully. Very goofy and I'm glad I saw them. Here came a grownup. Oops, I scurried back to the path. "You are so weird," Ray shook his head. We continued our walk and exited the fenced area. I felt relieved.

The afternoon zoomed by and we'd covered a lot of territory. Standing in front of a directory, Ray contemplated our choices. "Mm, we haven't seen the wombat yet. This way." We roamed up a new path and arrived just in time for another ranger

128

demonstration. In his speech, the ranger hit all the fine points I needed to know. "The wombat is fierce. When we bring him out, do not approach him from the front. The line forms to the right and you can take a picture from the side. Do not try to touch the wombat. DO NOT LOOK THE WOMBAT IN THE EYE."

I looked around. No one else was trembling. No one looked the least bit nervous. Folks were shuffling into line, willing sheep to the slaughter. Don't stare down the wombat. Shit. Why would they present such a creature to the public, putting everyone at risk? I was waiting for a cage to roll out, perhaps a creature strapped down like Hannibal Lector in *Silence of the Lambs*. The wombat needed to be trussed.

Instead, there was a ranger with the wombat in his arms. Folks did give a fairly wide berth as the line began to move by the wombat. Dark brown, it resembled a bear. Had an odd snout like nose and almost a flat forehead. The fur looked long and bristly. No need to pet this creature. The wombat appeared as if he'd been into the koala's eucalyptus stash. He didn't bare teeth or claws. There was no chance of eye contact since the wombat sat rather comatose on the ranger's lap. Ray participated, walked the line, and took his side angle picture. I stayed back and watched the crowd pay hush respects to the wombat. Finally, we had our brush with danger, but we didn't stare it down. We averted our eyes.

Chapter 20: The Workplace is Going to the Dogs

"Yap, yap." Oh great. Nothing will get done today. Sure enough, Becky the boss's wife who does some receptionist work brought Harry again. It's a spoiled rotten gray Scottish terrier. Cute enough face, but it's a yapper and quite distracting to the work environment. Of course, I'm the only employee who thinks that.

"Hey, Harry."

"How ya doin' boy?"

I hear Harry's progress from the lobby, down the hall, and I know where he's headed. Cupboard doors slam in the kitchen area, along with the rustle of a bag.

Sandra calls to him, "Harry, I have treats." He turns up his nose and trots onward, intent on his destination. Think of the theme from *Jaws* and that slow buildup of dread it inspires.

I get up to retrieve a file, think about closing my door, but it's too late. Harry rounds the corner to my office and heads straight for my leg. He barks once and jumps up, pawing at my legs. I try

130

to shake him off, to no avail. Sandra laughs. "Just pet him once and he'll leave. He wants attention."

"No, I'm not working at an animal shelter. I've got payroll to process. Get him out of here."

She bends down, treat in hand. "Ignore that mean accounting lady, Harry."

Now everyone congregates at my office. Babies and dogs, they're a magnet. Allan, Becky's husband, co-owner of Quorum and software engineer, and Harry's dad stands with coffee cup in hand. A bemused look on his face, he talks tough, but we all know Becky rules that roost. Rick, the other co-owner and RF engineer, arrives with another treat. He is an agitator and teases Harry with the biscuit. "Jump, fella. Over here, over here." Harry growls and leaps for it. He snaps at Rick's hand. Rick pulls back, startled, and he rubs the red spot where the dog's teeth scraped. Serves him right. I sit back at my desk, "Everyone, out of here. I'm doing payroll." I hate when the dog is stirred up. Makes me very nervous.

Becky corrals her dog and carries him to the front desk. Everyone wanders off to his stations. In about an hour, I buzz Becky with a question. No answer. I can use the exercise and I amble up front. She's outside so Harry can take care of his business. That dog has a bladder the size of a pea. I watch as he frolics a bit and she's in no hurry. Finally, they come to the door. Harry attempts to befriend me again. I ignore him and he slouches to his bed. Yes, she brings his special cushion and toys for his day at work. Ugh. By this time, I forgot

131

why I came up front and I stand there until I think of it.

"Do you have the shipping paperwork ready for Tecnavia?"

Becky rummages around the desk. Short blonde hair, button nose, twinkling brown eyes (she resembles Annette Bening) she's fun and nice, but not organized. She only comes in twice a week and the desk is chaos within an hour of her arrival. "Um. Here's the invoice." I glance at it, point out a few typos, and tell her I also need the customs documents. "Give me an hour." Harry sniffs in my direction and I retreat to my office.

The phone rings and rings and finally the overhead dinger resounds. Wondering what Becky is doing, I pick up. Mr. Lee from Singapore. I put him on hold and look for Allan. Great, now he AND Becky are outside with the dog. I wave him in to take his call. Not a whole lot is being accomplished at Quorum.

The door is open to the warehouse and I decide to at least pack up Tecnavia's gear. I switch on the foam machine and stick my head out the back door. Sandra's on smoke break and we chitchat. Tap-tap, I hear the click of Harry's nails on concrete and his little nose pokes out the door. That's my cue to leave. Back in my office, I enter some purchase orders, and then I decide the foam machine should be warmed up. I box Tecnavia, nag Becky again for paperwork (she's now headed to lunch with Allan and Harry), and check in the lab with Rick who asks, "Where's Harry? He hasn't been back here to visit me."

132

"Oh good Lord. The family's gone to lunch. Guess they didn't invite you." With that, I return to my office. Once Becky is back, I leave for lunch to run some errands and grab a burger. Back in an hour, I sense a weird vibe in the air. Rick pokes his head out of the kitchen and then lopes off to the lab without a word. Sandra, at her lab bench, doesn't shout out, "Where'd you go for lunch?" That was strange.

I enter my office and look around. No papers askew, nothing new in the in box, no red light on my phone indicating messages. I've got good ears and could hear giggles down the hallway. Here comes Harry again, straight towards me and under the desk. I leap up and Sandra is at the door howling. I peer under and Harry is enjoying kibbles. Now, I'll never be able to keep him out of my office.

"The look on your face was worth it," Sandra crowed. "Hey, Rick. We got her."

"Oh man, I wanted to see," Rick laughed. Even Allan and Becky, proud parents, had to come stand in my doorway and watch Harry devour his treats. Meanwhile, I fume.

"Not funny."

"Yeah, it was."

I busy myself to stifle a spurt of tears. I feel stupid because they put me on the spot. I can take a joke, but for me this is serious. I don't want a dog in my office, eating at my feet, and otherwise sniffing around. They just don't get it. Big or little, dogs scare me. I vow to leave next time it was "bring your dog to work day". That'll show 'em.

133

Fortunately UPS hollers from out back and everyone scatters. I sign for packages and finally, with corrected paperwork, seal up Tecnavia's box and hand it over.

Annoyed at everyone, I plow through the day and don't talk anymore. I generate reports, bustle around inventory, and act a bitch. Sandra knows I am pissed. She pops her head into my office to ask innocuous questions. She makes a point of forwarding a joke. No mercy. I don't yield and leave early without goodbyes.

Almost a year goes by. Around Christmas, Harry proudly wears the Santa sweater Sandra gives him. The jingle bell announces his location. Bah humbug. Finally, come spring, Allan buys Becky a stable to manage, so she is on to her horse heaven project. No more dabbling as a receptionist. I figure I am free from weekly Harry visits.

Alas, I spoke too soon. Becky travels to Montana for a week. Becky flies to Florida, and so on. Thus, Allan arrives to work with Harry in tow. This big burly man, with premature white hair, kowtows to a dog. Forget a 9 am start time; it's 10 am. Harry must sleep in, the lazy thing. Then treats, walks, lunchtime, nap, walks, and leave at 4 pm, not 5 or beyond. I guess Harry wants to avoid traffic. Allan should take vacation. I never see him write a lick of software.

To make my life worse, Sandra decides to bring in her puppy. So pug ugly, it is cute, her newborn sleeps all day and doesn't dare venture to my office. Sandra carries it outside to pee. I never see its feet touch the ground. Fortunately the puppy novelty wears off or maybe something is said to Sandra and Biscuit is uninvited to the office. A dual standard can be implemented at a privately owned corporation.

Kibbles are not placed under my desk again. I have some power. Supplies Sandra requests take extra long to purchase in that month she tortured me. She isn't happy when her exacto blades dulled and there were no replacements. I shorten my hours on the days Allan brings Harry. He never says a word about my silent protest.

I read about companies who encourage folks to bring their pets once a month. It's said to be good for morale. Yeah, but how about production? My bet (and I'm in the minority) is the numbers have gone to the dogs.

Chapter 21: A Bunny Explosion

Bunnies are harmless except when they eat Ray's fresh strawberries before he gets a chance to pick them from the garden. Then that white cottontail scampering about our backyard is a nuisance. Never saw his mother or any siblings. Instead, this teensy baby rabbit scoots fearlessly about our backyard. He grows quickly and now bounds between the back shrubs and the shed. His fat brown body can squeeze under the wood frame and Ray hasn't tampered with his narrow hide-a-way hole.

Out for a swim or to trim bushes, I can be within feet of him before he acts a tad nervous. He's not rabid or skittish and hasn't caused a mess in the backyard. I think he feels the same about me. I'm not rabid and while I do jump a bit if I don't expect him to leap out when he does, I haven't caused Mr. Bunny harm. He hates the whir of the lawnmower and ventures under our fence and to the field to escape the noise. If we don't see him for a while, Ray and I will comment, "Wonder if the hawk got him?" Indeed, high above us, perched on the telephone pole and then lazily

136

circling the field, two massive birds keep an eye out for dinner. Mr. Bunny should maintain a code red lifestyle and remain on high alert. Then, just when we think he's gone, I hear a rustle in the bushes and see the flash of his white tail. I'm surprised he hasn't gone a'courting to bring back a new bride. I think he's got it too good here and doesn't want to share.

So, am I gushing too much? You're thinking I've succumbed to raising rabbits. Absolutely not! Coincidently, Ray raised rabbits back in his teen days as a member of FFA (Future Farmers of America). That was enough for him. Now, back to me. I don't have any childhood horror stories about rabbits. I love Easter time and singing about Peter Cottontail. Always fond of Beatrix Potter books, I like children's bunny stories. I remember a favorite from the local library called *Naughty Bunny.*

Neighbors behind us had rabbits in a huge cage and they were fine to look at. I understand rabbits are messy, but that wasn't my problem. I would actually stick a carrot through the cage for the rabbits to sniff and eat. No loud noises, no raucous behavior, no escapes and marauding through the neighborhood terrorizing kids on bikes. Bunnies are endearing.

Thus it pains me to share two sad rabbit tales. Back in the early 1990s, I worked for Bridge 3Com – RF Division and the office was in a typical one-story development in North Dallas. Brick building, one scrawny tree out front, and the usual shabby shrubbery, but at least there's greenery to promote employee health and wellbeing. Each week, the

Hispanic landscape crew fired up all equipment and mowed, chopped, and edged in an hour. No thought or care was put into the effort. The little men chattered in Spanish, blared their music, and blew grass clippings into open car windows.

One lovely spring day, the office crew all heard the fateful twang of the weed eater and the sputter of the engine as it stopped. At the same time, our receptionist, Candice, shrieked, "Oh, they killed the bunnies." She ran to the bathroom in tears. Several engineers came up front and then walked outside to make sure the lawn crew was going to clean up the bloody splatter on the glass. Sandra and I arrived at Candice's desk, saw the mess at her window, and followed her to the bathroom. She was distraught and wouldn't leave the room until reassured that the blood reminder was gone. Whatever possessed the mother rabbit to have a nest at an office building? Good phone reception or pizza delivery choices? Either way, it was a fateful mistake and the whole bunny family was wiped out.

My second sad tale involves the hawks I mentioned. Ray never traveled much for his job, but he did attend the annual Electronic Distributors' Vegas show each year. I went once and that was enough, so in subsequent years I'd have a few days to myself. There was a brief time span when anything that could go wrong did go wrong while Ray was in Vegas. Principals called. Truant officers called. I'd deal with school issues. I'd handle equipment or car failure. Ray would leave for a fun convention and holy hell broke loose. We got past that and had several good years of no strange occurrences.

Then I arrived home one sunny May afternoon. Dropped my purse on the counter, leafed through the mail, and then looked out the kitchen French doors. Something was on the patio near the steps at the pool's shallow end. I walked outside, looked around, and hesitantly approached the thing. Flies buzzed and ants scurried. Sure enough, there'd been a bunny explosion. Other than blood and guts, all that was recognizable was tufts of a white cottontail. The hawk won and left his cruel mess on our patio. Nature is gross and Ray was gone. Fortunately, Chris lived in nearby apartments. I called and between classes he came over, wielded a shovel, hosed things down and restored beauty to our backyard.

Bunnies still scamper between the field and our backyard. Hawks circle above waiting for one fatal timing mistake. For the bunnies, it's a delicate balance to slip under the fence, bound over our small woodpile, skirt the pool, and find safe haven under the shed. Oh, and perhaps stop for a strawberry snack along the way.

Chapter 22: Benji Loves Aunt Joanne

"Did you tangle with a barbed wire fence or lose a duel?" I asked Linda when she answered her door. Scabby red streaks slashed her white arms, and one rapier thin whiplash cut diagonally down her cheek from the corner of her eye. Her short brown hair could not hide the carnage. I winced for her as I stepped inside. She tugged down her sleeves and shut the door against the chilly fall wind. It was late afternoon on an October Friday. We had both decided to knock off work early, have some dinner, and visit. I handed her my usual, a tin of brownies.

"It's my new boy, Benji." Linda said with a downcast look. Her long lashes swept her cheeks. "He didn't want to go to the vet to be de-clawed."

"Yikes. It looks like he definitely needs that." I replied. "Mmm, what smells so yummy?"

"A new Italian chicken recipe. You're my guinea pig. Well, the deed's not done yet," she said as she shuffled to the kitchen. "I couldn't get Benji in his cage. Cecil will have to take him."

"Nice slippers," I commented as we stepped around a large empty metal box. She had huge black kitty cats on her feet.

"I tossed off the heels the minute I walked in the door." She shoved the cage into a corner. "This was a great idea."

I set down my purse and also dumped some magazines on her kitchen bar. My head swiveled as I looked for the wild beast and prepared for him to pounce. Linda noticed and shook her head.

"You need to meet Benji before you judge him too harshly. He was scared and I'm clumsy. You'll love him, he's a good-looking cat, but he's hiding right now. He'll strut out later to visit."

I met Linda less than a year after I moved to Texas and changed jobs from traveling sales to an inside customer service position. Linda, Kathy, and Kearny were all hawking electronic components for a distributor back in 1981. Though we've since followed different paths and two moved out of state, these women are still a core group of my friends, and (I don't hold it against them) animal lovers. Linda is the cat lady, and she anointed me Aunt Joanne for her succession of pets. Linda claims she understands my fear of animals because she's not keen on dogs. However, there's a seed of doubt, too. How can I not want to adore and pet the kitties? She basks in her felines, shares stories, has pictures, and loves for them to loll on her bed.

Major Money and Jaguar were the Mutt and Jeff of cats. M.M. was the size of a panther, coal black, luminous green eyes, and long, long plush hair. At eighteen pounds, he looked like a black football on legs. Jaguar was as sleek as her name suggests and her purr rivaled any foreign motor. A delicate gray and white cat, she tolerated Major and vied with him for Linda's lap. Both cats ran her condo and immediately leaped onto any chair or couch I chose to sit in. That is the rule for cats. Both cats also emerged from slumber to parade through a room and walk between my legs. Could be coincidence, but it was me they chose to visit. Snub everyone and wait for me to shower adoration. Linda was generous in her apologies and she would lift them away and settle them into her lap. Sooner or later, they'd squirm out of her grasp, stroll the couch, leap a table or two, and nudge me or walk across my lap, dare to stop and plop down. Despite open arms and encouraging words from other cat-loving friends, Major and Jaguar sought my company.

They were lovely cats and I'm glad Linda enjoyed them. If I had to return to this world as an animal, a Linda cat would be a prime choice. Comfy conditions, top notch food, health care, a bed in front of the television, and an owner at my beck and call. Lots of children in this world don't get this level of care. Nonetheless, they are cats and they hiss. They could bite, scratch, or otherwise be wild. I contend that you never know what an animal is really thinking or what it might do.

142

I prefer to keep my distance. This is a difficult task as a cat magnet of sorts. Black pants and Joanne attract cats and cat hair. Whether I sit or stand or lean against a kitchen counter, a kitty will insinuate himself into my space. It will rub, slink, or cajole with a purr. I am immune to the pressure. I do not bend down to pick up or pet a cat. It is not in my nature and that drives cats berserk.

Linda did not evolve into a crazy cat woman with too many mouths to feed. She married Cecil in 1989 and, though he protested mightily, his marriage vows acknowledged a household of two cats, Jaguar and Cooper (Major Money had lived to a ripe old age and moved on to cat heaven). If by some chance, a kitty went missing, not one but two would replace the original. It was in Cecil's best interest to keep Linda's babies alive and well. Hence his midnight climb to the top roof beam of their new home to rescue a cat that managed to seek adventure up there, but then meowed in fear after peering down. Cecil built a special size swinging entrance door at the patio so the cats could roam outside at their whim. He designed a kitty litter removal system so as to streamline the cleaning process through a garage portal. In public, Cecil muttered, "I wish I had a dog," and portrayed himself as the put upon husband. In private, he watched TV with a cat tucked under an arm.

Jaguar became ill and Cecil drove her to the vet emergency. He helped Linda during Jaguar's kitty chemo, and ultimately mourned the loss of Jaguar too. Ready to get a new friend for Cooper, Cecil was surprised when Linda declined the offer.

She was fine with one cat. Regal Cooper, with his long gray coat, white face and white paws, lived the life of an only child. He'd been the loner, preferring to be viewed from afar. Now Linda sought him out to sit in her lap. Cooper beseeched Cecil to get him a sibling so he could return to his life of quiet luxury and naps under the bed.

Thus, unbeknownst to Linda, Cecil put out the word that he wanted a cat, not a kitten. He and Linda were getting older and didn't want to go through the baby phase again. Benji, the son Cecil never had (all the other males had been coddled mama's boys), a wayward adolescent orphan full of vigor, arrived as a ten year anniversary present and immediately scratched his new parents.

Linda bustled about the kitchen. We chatted as she pulled out plates, silverware, and placemats. I hoisted myself up on a maroon bar stool and let my shoes slip off my feet. The phone rang and Linda, seeing the caller I.D. excused herself to take a business call. I plucked a decorating magazine from her pile and leafed through it, idly munching on some nuts.

"Ah!" I jerked my left foot and looked down. Cooper brushed by my chair, his fluffy tail tickled my exposed leg above the sock. He blinked and sauntered out of the room, mission accomplished.

I decided to get up and peer into the oven. Ten minutes left on the timer and the dish sizzled. Garlic steam met my nose and my eyes teared up from onions. My stomach rumbled. Linda always joked that we could order pizza, but her cooking experiments never failed to impress. Since her phone call sounded like it was winding down, I poured us each a glass of wine and carried hers into her office. She rolled her eyes, flapped her hand as a sign that the caller was yak yakking, and sipped the wine. I went back to my kitchen perch and resumed my read.

A tap on my shoulder, then my forearm signaled I had a visitor. I swiveled to face Benji, a large green eyed, gray/black tiger striped cat. He was formidable. His paw touched my arm again as if he wanted to shake hands. No claws, merely a pat. He leaped from his chair to my lap. Thud. Fifteen pounds of cat spread out in all his glory. I'm never prepared for this and awkwardly attempt to shoo him away. Linda rounded the corner and clapped her hands, "No, Benji. Get down. I'm so sorry." She scurried over but Benji bounded to the floor and with a flick of his tail eluded her grasp and escaped out the cat door.

"That was Benji," Linda waved her hand toward the retreating cat. "He didn't scratch you, did he?"

Normally elusive, Benji appears if I visit. He's been Cecil's son and refuses Linda's lap to go sit by his father. Stirring up trouble with Cooper, Benji fights at mealtime, as if he won't get fed enough, and splashes the water bowl. A surly teen, he stays

145

out late and refuses to listen to Linda's entreaties. Like any proud father, Cecil keeps a bulletin board tally of Benji's successes. So far, three birds, two mice, and a snake are Benji's contribution to the household. To this, I say, "Yuck."

He's feisty and I'm wary, but he's never scratched me. Benji loves his Aunt Joanne

Chapter 23: Dogged Pursuit

"Do you have any pets?"

That's a logical chitchat question. Mingle at a cocktail party, or wait for a class to start; someone initiates conversation and the inevitable twenty questions. Married? Kids? Pets? No to the first two receives a shrug, no to pets is pursued.

"I own a dachshund named Friedrich Wilhelm III. Any dogs or cats?"

My insides squirm. I hesitate, "Um, no. Never really had an interest."

"You're kidding? How about fish?"

At this point, the room hushes, a spotlight blinds me, and I stutter. I spill my guts, confess my shame and spend the balance of time apologizing. "Well...I'm kinda afraid of animals...dogs, cats, fish, fowl...not keen on any."

People are astounded. I don't appear deranged. I explain further, "My mother didn't care for animals and she instilled her fear in me."

Excuses work if your mother drank, was a druggie, paranoid schizophrenic, or claimed an eating disorder. That's almost cool now. The animal fear thing, dismissed with an upraised

147

eyebrow. Folks are positive they can convert me to love their pet. Some are cat owners who don't care for canines. The dog lovers despise cats and understand my distaste for felines. But, how can I not love their chosen species? That's a challenge. In addition, friends acknowledge their pet is unhinged. "You'll love him anyway. Listen to this wacky act."

"Oh, you'd fall for my (fill in the blank – sheepdog, Siamese cat, elephant, tiger, boa constrictor)." Then my newfound friends proceed to discuss attributes, foibles, diseases, surgeries, diet, and sleep habits of their beloved pets.

I met Joanie and Helen in seventh grade English. Joanie lived up the block from the junior high so her home became the hangout. We'd troop in after school and Mrs. Marcolina barely raised an eyebrow. "Hello, girls. How was school?" a cigarette in hand, she greeted us in the kitchen and offered snacks. The aroma of spaghetti sauce swirled out of bubbling pots. This thin gray-haired Irish woman married an Italian and became one with pasta.

We'd jostle around the dining table, gulp a soda, and munch on cookies or Tastykakes and there'd be a thump, thump against the sliding glass door to the backyard. Bourbon, an Irish setter, hurled himself against the door, eager to be part of the action. The glass was a smeary mess from the dog's constant assault. "My Dad named him

148

Bourbon," Joanie told us, "because even as a puppy he looked drunk all of the time."

Sure enough, this fiery redhead was loopy. He'd leap, bound, and zigzag around the yard interfering with croquet or volleyball games. Tongue hanging out, Bourbon loped full tilt into a pole, tree, lawn chair or people. He acted like a drunk with no inhibitions, a crazed fool eager for attention. Try as I might to stay out of his way, Bourbon slimed me on a few occasions and the spittle droplets clung. No matter how hard I wiped, the slobber lingered and I'd excuse myself to the powder room to furtively dampen a towel and wipe the offensive spots. No teeth marks, just a splash of spit. I loved going to Joanie's but preferred indoor or front-yard activities.

Junior high was a time to meet new people and Joanie, Helen, and I added Trish to our crew. A petite pixie with blonde wavy hair, Trish was our athlete. She danced, clogged, and urged us off our sedentary butts. Usually, we met at Joanie's place for any activity. By high school, Trish and I worked at a Fayva shoe store. Friday night, Helen, in her yellow Mustang, picked up Joanie then would swing by to get Trish and me. This worked out great. Once in awhile, on a Saturday, we'd pick up Trish at her house, a daunting proposition.

First we'd pull up in Helen's car and wait, in hopes Trish opened the front door ready to go. Nope. We'd look at each other. Like Musketeers, we stuck together as a team. Up to the door and before we'd ring the bell, mad insane barks ensued as well as loud thumping. The front door bowed in

149

and out, like a cartoon scene. A head peered from the curtain. Not Trish's sisters. No it was a dog's head. Huge Great Danes, two of 'em ruled this house. Helen's and my legs shook like the Cowardly Lion approaching the Wizard of Oz. Even Joanie, accustomed to wacky Bourbon, feared the Danes. They were enormous. I never, ever sat on the living room couch. The dogs towered over us all, or stooped to look face to face, daring us to move. You could have saddled those two and rode them around the block. "Oh, they're pussy cats," Trish laughed when she'd find us cowered in the middle of the living room. Biggest pussycats I ever encountered. Needless to say, thank God Trish got her own vehicle and met us for dinner in town.

A neighborhood friend, Debbie, owned one collie when I met her in sixth grade. Major was a beautiful dog, like Lassie, and he looked smart. Well trained, he gave a sharp deep bark when I pedaled up the driveway. However, once Debbie came out, said, "No" to Major, he shut up and ignored us. Then another collie joined the family. Well, that was one more too many for me. This one didn't listen to instructions and barked constantly. I found it unnerving. There's a solution to every problem. "Hey, Debbie, why don't you come over to my house to hang out?"

Still dog lovers, Debbie and family now have three or more German shepherds. I lost count since I was paralyzed with fear at my one Christmas visit. Never did sit down. The dogs weaved in and out of the living room chairs, circling Debbie, her mother, and me. A low growl hummed. Unlike the purr of a cat, this sound did not signal contentment. Petrified, I extended a hand to pass over some pictures and the dogs glared at me.

Can't you put them outside? In another room? Down in the basement? I tried to send silent brainwaves, but the dog power prevailed. "It's cold out so the dogs stay in," Debbie said. Weren't German shepherds outside guard dogs tromping through the snow during World War II? What do you mean, they don't go outside on a sunny December day? I stood and talked faster. Debbie attempted to herd the dogs into another room, but they ignored her. "Cheryl's the one who controls the dogs, but she worked late last night and is asleep." By this time, my standing was awkward. Does this mean that if they went for my throat, only Cheryl's command could save me?

"Wow, I really need to get going. So good seeing you." No sudden movements. I eased on my coat and oozed towards the door, letting Debbie run interference on the dogs. Never did turn my back and I escaped with all parts intact. Whew!

Off to college with minimal animal encounters, other than a few frisky frat boys. As a business major, I even avoided dissection lab. Thus

151

I did not deal with animals, dead or alive. I commuted so missed out on roommates with cats or dogs. I led a sheltered life under the roof of George and Juanita Crowther, our own family non-pet cult. My brother had allergies and my sister drank from the fear-of-animal well along with me. Perhaps it does incubate and soon there's no cure.

Graduated from Temple University in 1980, and hired to sell gas pumps in Texas and Oklahoma. Excited to be on my own, I packed up and moved into an apartment in Arlington, Texas to begin adulthood. It was a whole new world to conquer and while I changed jobs from pumps to electronic parts, I stayed settled in my digs. My roots, history, and good friends were in North Wales, PA, and I added a new tier of friends in Texas. That, of course, meant I was fresh meat for friend's pets.

"Charlie's psycho." That's how I was introduced to Kathy's baby. Indeed this black cocker spaniel had been inbred one too many times. He had crazy eyes, barked incessantly, and bit Kathy on numerous occasions. She was good about keeping Charlie in another room when she had friends over. Nonetheless, Charlie remained ever present with his door scratching and howls. Kathy excused herself from party chat when a loud crash echoed from Charlie's prison. "Bad boy," we'd hear muffled. She'd come out, find a leash and go back in. Doggie downers were a viable solution. Charlie lived a really long time, too and remained nuts to the end.

"She loves you. If you pet her, she'll leave you alone." I find that's not the case. One tentative hand stroke and a creature wiggles for more. It's never enough. A cute child lisps a song, basks in applause, and launches into another round. The parents whisk the kid to bed before it becomes tiresome. No such luck with pets. The tolerance level is limitless. "Oh, they just want to see you. Yes they do, yes they do." Even worse, owners resort to baby talk.

It's the way of the world and I manage to enjoy new friends, play the "meet the pet" game without screaming, and sigh. I try not to gape in horror when, at my sister-in-law's house, Angel scampers on the top of the couch and stops to lick Bobby's bald head. At a party, I avoid food displayed in reach of my friend's pet's nose and tongue. I shudder inwardly at the cat sashaying amongst hors d'oevres placed on a kitchen bar counter. I laugh at myself, wash my hands, and shake off a panting dog or two.

Chapter 24: Bubba

"Were you bitten?"

"No, but I fear an animal attack."

With that, folks regale me with a sordid tale of a real-life pit bull gone mad. Here's one such story told by a writer friend:

My daughter and I drove home from the grocery store. We live out from town, so we wound our way on country roads. Pretty day and we admired the wildflowers. "Look," Elise pointed out the window, her voice strained. "That dog, it's attacking a cow." I slowed and we watched in horror as a pit bull leaped on a brown cow. The cow mooed, plaintive, in pain, but we didn't know what to do. I honked the horn, but that did nothing. The dog tore ferociously at the cow, which now flailed on the ground. By this time, Elise cried and huddled in her seat, hunched over to avoid the scene. I dialed 9-1-1 and told dispatch our location. Sheriff arrived shortly, but it was too late. Dead cow in the field, pit bull gone, and two shaken females. He took our statement. I identified the cow and pit bull's owners.

Sure enough, I received a court summons and testified on behalf of the cow. The owner completed in depth research and organized plenty of neighbors as backup. Apparently that pit bull terrorized the entire county. This wasn't Bubba's first time in the doggy slammer.

I stayed for the verdict. The judge, a big old boy, drawled "Bubba done gone bad. The pit bull is remanded to the state. Damages to be paid in the amount of one thousand dollars."

I listened in horror to her story. Thank God, Bubba wasn't set free. However, this tale reinforces my fears. You never know what an animal can do. This was a seriously misbehaving family pet. Unlike me, other friends' reactions are dismissive. "It was an aberration, things happen; you can't worry about stuff like that. My pet would never do such a thing." I'm not reassured.

Chapter 25:Hey Stupid, the Baby's Crying

"Oh you'll love the Muff. She's practically human."

Yeah, yeah I thought to myself. Heard that one before and I prepared myself for the usual onslaught of leaping, pawing, barking, and slobbering dog. Boy, was I in for a surprise. Been in Texas for a year and worked at Solid State Electronics as a customer service peon. My boss, Kearny, invited her co-workers to a Memorial weekend picnic, so I drove from Arlington to Duncanville. In retrospect, Solid State was a crappy place of employment, but it yielded an amazing batch of friends. Even though career-wise we went our separate ways, we all stayed in touch, even after twenty years.

I was fairly new at Solid State and hadn't gotten a full sense of all the personalities. This picnic would be a good start. Kearny and her husband Paul, both late twenties, were the old married couple. They wed after college, he joined the Air Force, and she enjoyed the benefits of his station in Japan. Once he completed his service he

156

hired on at Delta and flew a ton of hours. They had a house in Duncanville, no kids yet, and were the picture of domesticity. Oh, and they had the Muff. This dog was their baby and Kearny insisted she was the smartest canine on earth. I, the animal magnet, hoped this genius wouldn't latch on to me at the picnic and follow me everywhere.

Wasn't the first person at the party; free food and beer ensured attendance. Arrows, along with the smell of charcoal, pointed to the fence gate and I entered the backyard. So far, so good. No barking. The dog must be inside. Kearny came over, accepted the flowers I gave her, and introduced me to Paul, an energetic Boston redhead, complete with freckles. Pale blue eyes, a wide smile, Paul oozed enthusiasm. He showed me the drink coolers, encouraged me to grab some snacks, and talked up a storm like we were old friends. "Excuse me, I've got to check my briskets. I'll also be cooking some burgers. Hope you're hungry," Paul said as he charged off towards a huge grill.

My stomach growled as I mingled amongst my co-workers and enjoyed the atmosphere of horseshoes, volleyball, or laziness. Temperature was in the 80s, so it wasn't too sweltering to move about. I wandered to the snack table and grazed on chips and Mexican dip. Kearny came up to refill a bowl. "So, you met the Muff?"

"No, I haven't even seen your dog." I mumbled with my mouth full.

"She's right here, under the table."

157

I bent down, past the checkerboard plastic tablecloth, and there was a small white curly haired dog, a mixed breed of sorts. She lounged in the shade, calmly watching the scene. Her brown eyes observed me, but she made no move to get up or seek attention. She might have yawned.

"Wow. She's pretty quiet considering all of the commotion." A spirited volleyball game raised the noise level.

Kearny nodded. "Muff's unique. She has her own routine, likes this shady spot, won't chase balls unless we prod her, ignores people if we've obviously allowed them in, Won't jump, bark, or be annoying."

"I'm impressed. I didn't believe you at work."

"She's a great pet and with Paul gone so much, I have someone to talk to who won't argue with me." Kearny pulled her blonde hair back and laughed.

I have to say I wasn't worried that this dog would decide to lick or chomp my leg. I didn't feel nervous or uneasy with her under the table. She exuded a studied indifference to everyone. She remained in her spot when we all filled our plates with meats, salads, and peach cobbler. Seated at a picnic table, Paul called her name and she paused as if to decide if it was worth the trouble to answer her master. Finally, Muff arose, stretched, and trotted over for a handout. She accepted the food but did not then circle the table, begging for more. No pestering, no yaps, no sniffing. Muff licked her chops and sought more shade. I'd never seen anything like it.

The picnic was only the first of many fun times in Duncanville. Kearny quit Solid State soon after that day, became pregnant, and remained a stay-at-home mother once Sarah was born. We were friends and enjoyed hanging out. Paul had a crazy flight schedule, so Kearny would invite me for dinner. I never hesitated, never thought about whether the dog would roam around and be a bother. Muff generally barked once when I'd ring the doorbell. It was a deep throaty bark for such a proper female, with a hint of whiskey and cigarettes. It sounded fierce enough to scare away a stranger. Muff stood guard by her owner's side. However, once Kearny let me in, Muff trotted away. She'd give an over the shoulder look, like "don't try any funny business."

Paul managed to be off work and home one Saturday night. Kearny had cabin fever, enough so that she entrusted me with the care of her babies. Dinner and a movie date. She and Paul would be gone for four hours at the most. "I'll have Sarah fed and she should sleep. If she wakes up crying, change the diaper. If she still cries, here's a bottle to warm up for her. It'll be easy."

I'd never done much babysitting and it had been quite awhile since I'd changed a diaper. What the heck? I could keep the kid alive for four hours. Now the thought crossed my mind and I asked, "What about Muff? Is she going to be okay with me there, but you and Paul gone?"

"Sure, no problem. She knows you and we'll tell her to be good. Isn't that right, Muff?" Kearny addressed the dog that stood contemplating our

159

faces. She knew something was up. "Let her out when she stands at the sliding door. She won't make any messes inside."

"Okay. Well, have fun and don't worry. We'll all be fine here." I worked to reassure myself. Kearny and Paul skedaddled out the back door and then I heard the garage door go down.

Muff stood in the kitchen and stared at me. With a shrug that said, "Rookie," she walked over to her daybed to lie down.

I tiptoed down the hallway to peer into Sarah's room. I heard a snuffle and that was it. Kid's breathing, we're off to a good start. I eased out, pulling the door closed, and went back to the living room to watch MTV, back when they actually showed videos. I didn't have cable, so this babysitting gig wasn't too bad.

Zoned out, I started when Muff gave a low, quick bark. My focus now away from the television, I saw her standing at the sliding door. Again, she gave a quick bark and looked at me with disdain. I'm sure if she had something to throw at me, she would have. Duh, I was slow on the uptake. Finally, I remembered and got up to open the door. She scooted outside, took care of business and came back in. With a final glare in my direction, Muff settled down.

As long as I was up, I roamed into the kitchen for a soda and snack. Kearny had pointed out some goodies and I wanted a slice of chocolate cake. A little tap-tap of nails and the pad of paws let me know Muff had followed me. She sidled over to her bowl and lapped up some water.

160

Nonetheless, she tracked my movements, ready to report any misbehavior. Cake plate in hand, I returned to the couch. Muff retraced her steps, turned three times, and curled into a ball.

I clicked channels and relaxed, with another hour or so to go. Again, Muff gave a low bark. She now stood up, looked at me, and sauntered towards the hallway. "Hey, stupid. The baby's crying." The dog said it all with one look then added, "And wipe that crumb from the corner of your mouth." Sure enough, I heard a bleating cry, then a wail.

"I'm coming, I'm coming." I picked Sarah up and she lowered her tone from siren level to not quite ear-splitting. The diaper change wasn't too nasty, and she started to kick her legs happily and even smiled. Muff, meanwhile, stayed underfoot protectively eyeing the child. A fresh scream commenced, so I hauled Sarah to the kitchen with me, retrieved the bottle, zapped it briefly, and plunged it into the sound maker. That shut her up and she slurped the milk, little fists waving in the air. Muff, overseeing the whole operation, appeared happy with the quiet result and returned to her spot on the living room floor.

That said, in came Kearny and Paul. She scooped Sarah out of my arms and asked, "Is she okay? Did you have any trouble?"

"Everything's fine. Changed her diaper and now you see, she wanted the bottle. Otherwise, no problem. Did you two have a good time?"

"It was so amazing to get out. We needed that." They did look happy and refreshed. I grabbed my cake plate to put in the sink, turned off the TV, and said my goodbyes. Muff walked with all of us to the door, and gave me one final human look. This one said, "I was in charge tonight, and you woefully executed your duties. I could report you, but I won't. Next time, no remote control for you."

Chapter 26: Animal Shenanigan Entertainment

Roadrunner eludes the Coyote and I laugh with glee. *Underdog, Scooby Doo, and Pinky and the Brain* are welcome in my house. They can beep-beep, explode, do double takes, or "plot to take over the world." I love it. I watched my share of *Mr.Ed* as a kid, laughed at Arnold the pig on *Green Acres*, and cheered for *Lassie* to save the day. Now that I think about it, my mother did not join us kids in front of the television. Dad liked Roadrunner, Bugs Bunny, Daffy Duck's slow fume, Mickey Mouse, Goofy, and the gang - we giggled at all of these character's antics. They weren't real. They didn't slobber, bite, or bare teeth. Oh, they might have carried a firecracker or two, but that's harmless fun.

Now let's look at the seamier side of animals on television. I'm referring to true life animal shenanigans. Currently, a huge feature on *America's Funniest Home Videos* is animal goofs. Dogs licking baby's face, any animal drinking from a toilet, a camel (at a wildlife park) with its head stuck in a car window slobbers seeking food. Grossly disgusting. Again there's a voice in my head saying, "Don't touch that, icky, stay away."

An aside: Truly, a drive-thru wildlife park is the petting zoo horror for adults like me. You are trapped. The animals roam free. You drive through poop. Large creatures surround and bump your car. Smudges, spit, and animal sweat smear your car windows and doors. The goal is to open your windows and "experience" nature with a bag of stinky feed that becomes a goo ball in your hand. All of that for the family package price of $34.99? No thank you.

I'll go to the zoo where animals are caged in some capacity. Even that's a bit dodgy these days. A gorilla escaped in Dallas and rampaged through the zoo, injuring quite a few people. In San Francisco, a tiger leaped from its habitat and mauled a man to death. These animals were agitated, provoked, and they did what came naturally. They lashed out. I don't blame the animals one bit. Yet it supports my argument, my inner fears – you don't know what an animal is going to do. Day after day, zookeepers, food specialists, animal trainers spend time with their captives. Nothing may happen, and then one day the creature maims or kills its caretaker. Huh? That wasn't in the plan. Poor Roy (of Siegfried and Roy in Vegas) let down his guard one day, and his favorite white tiger took a major swipe at him. You never know.

Back to television: There's the "Stupid Pet Tricks" segment on David Letterman's show. I avert my eyes and yet, peer through my fingers to watch in horror. The absolute worst trick imaginable was the man, who drank milk, opened his mouth, and let his dog lap it up. OH MY GOD! I gag as I think about it; must swish some Listerine in my mouth before moving on.

Now I was raised on plenty of nature shows. Mom chose to read in another room when my father happily tuned into *Wild Kingdom*. David and I would watch transfixed, horrified, but we hung tough with Dad. Another favorite, Jane Goodall; Dad was positively ape for her. Monkeys, chimps, and orangutans are amusing, and the shows held our attention. David would scratch himself, stick his butt in the air, and do the monkey walk. We'd laugh until Dad said, "Hush."

In elementary school, the science teacher rolled out the old projector, spent time threading the film, sent someone to the Audio Visual department to come help, and sooner or later the lights lowered. The clickety-clack of the whirring wheels lulled everyone into a stupor and we watched the latest *National Geographic* special featuring birds, lions, or creatures of the jungle. Boys howled along with wolves, and girls squirmed at the sight of snakes. I must have seen each film at least four times. By sixth grade, they were grainy and scratched, but hey, the showing killed time.

Today's high definition programs exaggerate every last drop of blood in a lion kill. No more shaky camera work or long distance shots. Instead we see nature detailed in splendor or horror. *Shark Week* on *Discovery Channel* has old-fashioned thrills and chills. On a big screen television, those dead-

165

eyed eating machines bump a boat or cage, and me, sitting at home in my lounge chair. Yikes. Animal Planet explores everything from prairie dogs to ants. The *Planet Earth* series is revolutionary in its camera work. Mesmerized, I watched a rare snow leopard tumble down a mountain to capture its prey. Then I observed the glowworms of New Zealand.

All fascinating, all appreciated. I can watch, keep my hands clean, and change channels if disturbed.

There are plenty of pleasant animal films. *Bambi* begins with a bang, but once Bambi flees the fire and loses his mother, that animated Disney flick introduces us to bouncy characters like Thumper and we all frolic in the woods together. *Lady and the Tramp* is memorable for its characters and a Peggy Lee song. Even as a kid, I wasn't immune to the charms of that scalawag Tramp or feared for Lady's life at times. I danced along with Baloo and buddies in *The Jungle Book*. When else but in a Disney animated tale would I enjoy a jungle adventure? Then again there was the tick-tock of the clock in the crocodile's stomach in *Peter Pan*. However, the odds of me in crocodile infested waters are zero.

Disney also featured real-life animal adventures and those were more forbidding. *Old Yeller*, sure it was a boy's love for his dog and the

166

loyalty of that creature, but there's that rabies issue. My mother's voice reverberated in my head.

As much as I don't want to ride a horse, I envied Elizabeth Taylor on Pie in *National Velvet*. See, it never ran for the trees to scrape her off. Or the scene in *The Black Stallion* when the boy, bareback on the gorgeous creature, leaps from the ship is glorious. It looks like great fun to gallop down a beach atop a fabulous black stallion, but again, only on film. I can imagine the reality of me on a recalcitrant nag, sand whipping everywhere, the horse stopping to pee, and finally dumping me, no doubt, on a sand bar.

Horse movies entertained me, books not so much. *Misty of Chincoteague*, kinda boring. I remember faking interest in *My Friend Flicka*, both the book and TV show. They never showed or described the horse peeing. Fictional horses didn't snap at the hero's leg or try to buck her off. Grooming a horse sounded like a lot of work and trouble to me. Guess I'm selfish, but I have enough trouble keeping myself clean and presentable for the world. However, junior high age girls are supposed to love horses, yearn to own a horse, and want to go to camp for horseback riding. I'd murmur in agreement when friends talked about horses, but managed to avoid camps at all cost. I was my mother's daughter, after all.

I liked plenty of animal books as a child. We owned the obligatory animal alphabet book and my favorite creature was a zebra. *Where the Wild Things Are, Curious George, Clifford the Big Red Dog* – all classics, all wonderful. Same with any Dr.Seuss

167

rhymes. Whether it was *Go,Dog,Go* or *Horton Hears A Who*, I was enthralled.

As an adult, I'm not keen on Lilian Jackson Braun's cat detective books. She's a beloved writer, she's popular, but I don't care about the owner or the cat or any cat descriptions. In general, as I read a work of fiction I tend to skip over long passages on a pet. Licking, romping, barking, rubbing a tummy. These are all activities I bypass. Pets do serve a purpose in plotlines. They always bring their owner back to the house to be fed or walked. Or owners are oblivious to danger until a pet barks, hisses, or squawks. I'll concede animals are useful in that regard. Then again, with a dog, because someone has to walk the darn thing, even at night, one is put into danger.

Whether it is in television, film, or literature, animals are a key aspect of entertainment. Folks love their creatures and consider them crucial to their lives. Thus, animals offer a foil, a lynchpin, and fodder for writers. It's ironic that I, a non-animal lover, write this book and no doubt capture animal lovers' attention. I'm distressed and yet compelled to tell tales of guinea pig treachery, feline friendship (attempted), and equine epistles. Animal shenanigans are impossible to avoid in this world.

Chapter 27: Animal Humanitarian Efforts
(You Never Have to Clean Up the Poop)

What to get my father for his birthday? He didn't need a thing. Besides, I lived fifteen hundred miles away, so shipping was inconvenient and expensive. Then I read a newspaper article about zoo adoptions. As a fundraiser and to promote animal awareness, zoos put prices on certain creatures and anyone may adopt a rare species.

I booted up the website and browsed. It all looked pretty easy. You made a selection, printed out a form, and mailed in the envelope with money. In return, you received adoption papers along with a photo of your new family member. You could visit it anytime during normal hours, plus the zoo held a party once a year for the adopter and adoptee. What could go wrong with an exotic animal behind bars, pictures, and cake? This was an anxiety-free animal interaction.

A single fee covered the one-year sponsorship. No extra money required for clothing or food. No health insurance needed. You didn't have to write a weekly letter, like you would for an adopted child in Malaysia. In turn, no notes sent home from teachers describing how your youngster doesn't work to potential, or phone calls in the middle of the night from the police saying your teen was arrested for underage drinking. Hassle free – simply pay a fee and lay claim to an exotic bird, fish, or monkey.

Baby pictures beckoned and these critters proved popular. "Sold Out" was stamped over the majority. I moved on to the surly adolescents. A black rhino was expensive, plus he wasn't smiling in his adoption photo. He looked like trouble. I decided to search for an animal that resembled my father since animals and owners do start to look alike over the years. My father is balding and his ears stick out; maybe that wasn't a brilliant idea.

The zoo manipulated me with photos of animals, all with huge woeful eyes determined to tug at heartstrings. Various fur balls gazed outward and pled for adoption, as if they wouldn't be fed their daily allocation of vitamins and minerals. I had a price range in mind and settled for a pygmy hedgehog named Winky. I preferred the name Sam, but I didn't want to confuse my new adopted sibling. I ordered him up for my father, who merely said thanks. Then I forgot about my new brother until the renewal notice arrived. I declined to re-up.

Turns out I've been usurped. Dad not only re-paid Winky's adoption, he insisted on upgrading his cage accommodations. Not only that, he sent

170

Winky on an all-expenses paid trip back home to Africa to see his family. Dad showed me a postcard he received that thanked him for the trip. Later, Dad mentioned he scheduled an appointment with his lawyer to review his will. Do I need to worry?

Chapter 28: I Can't Count Sheep; They Could Attack.

I dream about animals. A nature show on Discovery Channel feeds my nightmares for weeks and creates a muddle of paralyzing fear. I can't escape four-legged fur balls chasing me, be it a dog, a coyote, a leopard, or a bunny. It's all a mishmash of dream locations, time zones, and various years. One night, I'm a kid on a bike, legs churning faster as a creature roars behind me. Another evening, I'm with Ray at an exotic locale. In my dream, he waves farewell as I struggle feebly. A ferocious sea lion drags me away.

I open my mouth to scream. My voice evaporates against the gnawing, snarling, devouring, attacking, and howling. Blood streaming everywhere, my heart pounds. I want to wake up but can't. I'm held slave to my demons.

Disturbing dreams. I hear the flutter of wings. I awake and point to the ceiling. "It's there. Right there." I gesture but Ray turns over. "Go back to sleep, Joanne. It's a dream."

"No." I scramble out of bed and turn on the light. Ray squints and covers his eyes. I insist that he get up to whack the bat off the ceiling. He won't budge.

"You don't have your glasses on." Ray attempts to reason with me, muffled words from his pillow. "You can't see a thing. That's because there's nothing there."

I'm aware of his words, but my brain clouds with dream webs. My fear overcomes rational thought. I'm lost.

The non-bat wins. It gets to live. I turn off the light and climb back into bed. Unsettled tears burn my eyes, as Ray, unaware, gives me a half-hearted pat. The next morning he laughs but I'm angry. I'm also tired from flailing about in my sleep.

At least I'm consistent. Awake or dreaming, animals terrify me. Nothing has changed through the years. No cuddly animal dreams. No horseback rides on a windswept beach. No saving the whales project. I don't awaken eager to pursue a career in veterinary medicine. I toss and turn after watching the original film, *The Omen*. Damian, be damned. Those freakin' black dogs in the cemetery are my nightmare.

Sweet dreams for me have no animals in sight. Counting sheep is not an option.

Chapter 29: My Torturous Final Days on Earth

I'm parked in the sunroom along with twenty other residents. At the mercy of our nurses, activities are chosen for us and we attend. Those of us with no voice can't complain out loud. Yesterday we listened to lousy music. I wish my hearing were gone. Oh it's pleasant if someone plays the piano or spins some old Billy Joel tunes. Now that is music. Instead, the local high school band played a salute to *West Side Story*. Hasn't any other band music been composed?

But at ninety, this tiny twig of a person has no power. In my eighties, I could gesture, frown, or curse. I got away with so much when Ray was alive. He had opinions, but always deferred to mine.

After Ray passed on, I did okay by myself until I fell and broke my hip. I'd always joked I would end up living in my sister's basement. Ten years younger and a heck of a lot healthier I thought she'd outlive me. Lori promised she'd throw food down to me and offer beer with a straw. Well, she's gone too.

Ray's boys, Chris and Kevin, signed me into this home. That's fine. They're almost seventy and ornery. Without Ray we didn't have much in common, especially since the stroke took my voice and I can barely see.

I hear the click of heels and a clap of hands. Mrs. Davis, the activities director bustles into the sunroom. "Good morning everyone. We have a special treat today. I know it's been a while since we've done this, and for you new residents you are in for an excellent day. I want to introduce Shari Morgan from the local SPCA. Let's give her a round of applause."

In a singsong voice, Ms. Morgan tells us about our day. "I brought some of our best behaved kittens and puppies to brighten this Tuesday. Our animals will sit on your laps, cuddle, and make friends."

Oh good Lord. I am in hell. Take me now, please. I try to squirm in my seat. Nothing gives. I try to catch Nurse Loretta's eye and implore her to roll me out of here pronto. Nope, she's too busy clapping her hands and reaching for a kitten. Holy crap. She's bringing it to me. "Ms. Joanne, this is Whiskers. She's too sweet." With that, Whiskers is plopped on my lap. I can't move. I want to say, "Take this away. Shoo." I try to bat my eyes, shake my head, but it is useless. I'm a prisoner. The cat is now in my face. We make eye contact and it knows how I feel. Whiskers narrows her golden eyes, gives a barely perceptive nod, and turns her butt towards my face.

175

Nurse Loretta returns with a yellow Labrador, causing Whiskers to take shelter on my hunched shoulders. The cat paws my gown. The day deteriorates. To my relief, she plucks the darned cat from off my neck and gives it to the wizened old broad next to me. Her name's Trixie…no, Trendi. This bottled blonde woman, of course, spells Trendi with an "i".

Anyway, now I've got Bones panting in my face. I feel a rough tongue lick my cheek. The horrific creatures of my worst nightmares are thrust one after the other onto my lap. They stink, they drool, and I can't muster a fit. Please, God, strike me with a bolt of lightning.

This is my fate. I wonder what Mrs. Davis will plan for us next – perhaps a day of horse therapy or a trip to the petting zoo. I laugh maniacally to myself. Tears spring to my eyes. Nurse Loretta pats my shoulder. "Now, Ms. Joanne, no need for tears. We'll bring the animals back another day."

The End

About the author

Joanne Faries, originally from the Philadelphia area, lives in Texas with her husband Ray. She graduated from Temple University (BBA), and University of Texas-Arlington (MBA), but she should have pursued liberal arts. After years in office management, she was fortunate to leave the world of electronics, and pursue her writing dream. A part-time job as a documentation specialist for Omega Research keeps her in paper and pens. Published in *Doorknobs & Bodypaint*, she also has stories and poems in *Magnapoets* and *Silver Boomer anthologies*. Joanne is the film critic for the *Little Paper of San Saba* (a town without a cinema)

www.wordsplash-joannefaries.blogspot.com

www.joannefaries.com

Made in the USA
Charleston, SC
01 February 2012